ADVANCED AEROBATICS DOWN UNDER

Getting into a Pitts

DAVID J PILKINGTON

Copyright © 2023 David J Pilkington

All rights reserved.

ISBN: 978-0-9925974-8-1

DEDICATION

Ken McKechnie and Newton Sanbrook provided my first opportunity to get into a Pitts through the Australian Aerobatic Club Melbourne Chapter.

To my family: Jennifer, Catherine and Jackson.

CONTENTS

	Forward	i
	Acknowledgments	ii
1	Moving On	1
2	The Pitts	4
3	Pitts Checkout	12
4	Endorsement Questionnaire	29
5	Cesspit of Misinformation	42
6	Advanced Spinning	51
7	Train for the Unexpected	54
8	Snap Rolls	58
9	Complex Manoeuvres	61
10	Intermediate Competition	64
11	Low Level Aerobatics	70
12	Advanced Competition	73
13	Formation Aerobatics	81

FORWARD

Some 22 years ago I penned an endorsement for an aerobatic book written by Gene Beggs which was largely for Pitts Aircraft. I stated at that time that occasionally a book comes along that is a "MUST READ" book.

This book, Advanced Aerobatics Down Under by David Pilkington also falls into that category. It is a MUST READ, particularly for one contemplating flying a Pitts in one's future. It is informative, easy to read, and contains a wealth of knowledge not only about the airplane but also how to fly it.

Read it, absorb the material, and then read it again and again. Each time you will gain additional bits and tips that escaped you in your previous reads. Looking for a gift for that friend who aspires to fly Aerobatics? This is the perfect gift, one that he or she will treasure for a lifetime.

William B Finagin

Bill has kindly offered to write a chapter in this book on emergency recovery. For those who don't know him:

IAC hall of fame honoree 2008
Lifetime member of IAC and EAA
Commercial Pilot
Gold seal instructor
Flight instructor, MCFI-A
Single engine land and sea
Multi engine land
Rotorcraft-helicopter
Instrument airplane
Remote Pilot

David J Pilkington

ACKNOWLEDGMENTS

Cover design and photo by Kathy Mexted.
https://www.kathymexted.com.au/
Pitts S-2A photograph in the air by Kathy Mexted.
Pitts S-2A taking off by Phil Vabre.
Pitts S-1 in the air by Dale Castle.
Pitts S-2C just airborne by William B Finagin.
Images by David Hooke for general flying in a Pitts S-2C.
Images by Bruno Roque for an Advanced sequence in a Pitts S-2C.
Black & white image of Pitts by Rob Fox.
Images from NASA reports.

1 MOVING ON

Aerobatics, especially competition aerobatics is a challenging sport. There is always more to learn and more to do, much more to do. This book is aimed at those who have been flying a basic aerobatic trainer, perhaps a Super Decathlon for some time. Perhaps competed in Sportsman aerobatic competitions and ready to move up to the next level. You would have been through everything in my book, Aerobatics Down Under. In fact, I will assume that you are familiar with the content of that book, including the abbreviations used, as the starting point for this book.

You are obviously addicted to aerobatics now and it can only get more intense. The next step is the Intermediate competition level and you know that the aeroplane you're currently flying is not up to it. Time to look around at the options. Will you continue to rent an airplane or will you buy one, perhaps with a small group of friends?

There is a range of airplane types to consider but let's quickly get to the bottom line. Everyone agrees that the "most bang for the buck is a Pitts." Of course, they're generally referring to the purchase of a second-hand single seat Pitts. The Pitts has more competition when it comes to the two seat options however they are still generally a cheaper

option than the various monoplanes and certainly adequate to take you to the next level and beyond.

I first saw a Pitts in 1974, an S-2A which was flown by Chris Sperou to win Unlimited at the Australian Aerobatic Championships at Point Cook. Just amazing for someone who had only two years before learnt aerobatics in an Airtourer with 100 hp. I had my 1500 ft aerobatic approval in the Airtourer when I went to the UK to study for my Masters Degree at Cranfield in aerodynamics, design and flight test engineering. I saw the Rothmans Team fly their display many times in their Pitts S-2A aircraft and I was hooked – I just had to fly one but that had to wait until 1978.

There is quite a choice amongst Pitts too. How many seats do you want, or need? Do you intend proceeding beyond Intermediate into the Advanced Category too? Do you dream of getting into Unlimited Category. Of course, we all know the limitations of a tubby biplane in earning scores at top level competitions when up against the clean lines of a modern monoplane. It was for that reason that I built a monoplane, the Laser, with two friends back in the '80s and flew it in Unlimited aerobatic competition for many years. I saw Randy Gagne compete in an S-2S at the 1996 World Aerobatic Championships where he came 77th. A Pitts competed in the 2013 World Aerobatic Championships but was far from competitive. Robert Armstrong has also demonstrated how well a Pitts can score in Unlimited World Aerobatic Championships with his S-1C in 1992.

That S-1C is famous for Robert having painted the outline of ailerons on the top wing after being the butt of jokes. He also flew the S-1-11B in WAC 1996 and impressed many with his performance to come in at 30th place. Robert is also well aware of the scoring disadvantages and last competed in his CAP 231 in 2013.

Most of us have a limited budget so pay your money and take your choice, whether it be renting or purchasing. A small group is a good way of getting into ownership of a high performance aeroplane. Three reasonable and like-minded people getting together works very well. Fixed costs are split three ways so it becomes quite economical compared to renting a similar airplane.

Australia has more prescriptive requirements for aerobatics than most other countries but wherever you are in the world you will find the technical considerations to be relevant, even if only self-imposed. This book therefore details the specific Australian requirements as the basis.

2 THE PITTS

This is a very big subject as there are so many models and variants of the Pitts. Here I will stick with the certified factory models plus the S-1-11B as made by the factory. The two seat 200 hp S-2A was first produced in 1971 by Aerotek Inc in Afton. Curtis Pitts continued to own the type certificates and performed all the engineering, design and certification activities for the S-2A and the single seat S-1S. The S-1S commenced production in 1973. Kits for the homebuilt S-1E and S-2E aircraft were made available – per the plans they were identical to the original certified S-2 and S-1S, both with 180 hp and a fixed pitch propeller, however many owners altered the design, often to a great extent. Curtis sold his interests to the owner of Aerotek, Doyle Child, in 1977. In 1981, Frank Christensen bought the works and renamed it Christen Industries. That  brought the homebuilt Christen Eagle into the fold. With Curtis Pitts out of the business, the engineering design work was led by Herb Andersen who was also General Manager of the factory.

It wasn't viable to turn the Pitts S-2 into a certified Christen Eagle. The Eagle doesn't have any instruments in the rear cockpit and that was unacceptable to the FAA. If a second instrument panel was to be fitted then the mechanism for the robust Eagle canopy couldn't be accommodated. The spring aluminium main landing gear of the Eagle would've required significant effort to redesign and test to be approved for a certified airplane. However there was a significant set of design changes introduced for the Pitts S-2A in 1981 including the symmetrical ailerons with spades and the double bubble canopy. When I was Chief Engineer, and Vice President – Engineering in the mid-'90s I had the opportunity to directly compare the detail design of the Eagle with the Pitts. There were certainly some detail improvements in the detail of the Eagle, the fittings for the lower wing spar attachment spring to mind.

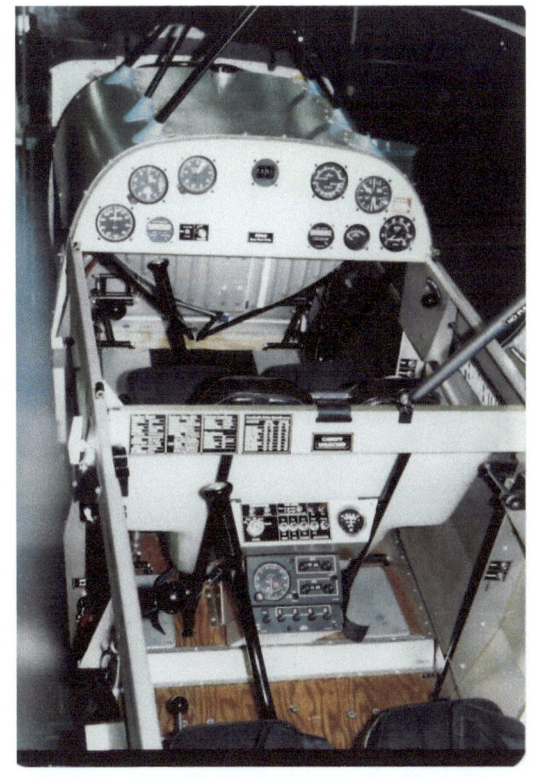

Along the way Herb found time to design and certify the Husky utility aircraft based on the Piper Cub design. It became the mainstay of factory production especially during the years when economic conditions meant that Pitts sales were slow.

The single seat S-2S was developed from the S-2A with the installation of a 260 hp Lycoming engine. The two seat S-2B then followed on from the S-2S in 1982. The Pitts S-1T with a 200 hp engine and constant speed propeller replaced the S-1S in production in 1981 and ceased production in 1995.

If you seek a single seat Pitts then my advice is to go for an S-1T as built by the factory – it is a very nice, high performing airplane. If your choice is one of the many Experimental homebuilt Pitts around then, before you buy, do significant research into the logbooks, ask around of people who have seen the airplane and get a good pre-purchase inspection. A lot of the owner-builder design alterations are far from being improvements.

Of course, Curtis went on to design the model 11, Super Stinker, which is owned by Aviat Aircraft Inc now and the model 12 with the Russian Vedeneyev M14P/PF radial engine of 360-400 HP which is available from Jim Kimball Enterprises, Inc.

I should mention Steen Aero Lab which took on the rights to the Pitts S-1C homebuilt and later developed the improved S-1SS plans and kits. They say the "S1-SS is similar to the certified S1-S "Roundwing" Pitts Special, but it uses the "Super Stinker" aileron technology developed by Curtis for championship-level aerobatic competition." Steen also offers the Pitts Model 14 powered by a 400 HP Vendenyev M14PF radial engine.

Steve Wolf has been prolific in developing Experimental variants of the Pitts biplane since 1978 and they are still popular to this day.

The S-2B remained in production with nil design changes until 1995 when I started work at Aviat Inc as Chief Engineer. Malcolm White had purchased the factory from Frank Christensen in 1994 and wanted to do a number of things differently. My first priority was the Husky to ensure that the business was viable as Pitts sales were low. There was a prototype of an aerobatic Husky part finished which was the project which really attracted me to Afton. However there was so much work to be done with Husky engineering that I had little time for the aerobatic airplanes.

Malcolm sold the business to Stu Horn in 1996 and renamed it Aviat Aircraft Inc. I became even more busy!

The S-1-11B story – a true Unlimited Category competition biplane. When the Super Stinker turned up at Afton, Stu arranged a brainstorming session with myself, Curtis Pitts, Robert Merritt, he was our prototype builder), plus another guy – Dan Clarke from memory. Lots of input so some bullet points from memory:

I am a crude aerodynamicist. If you want to roll faster so make the ailerons bigger. Everything about aileron design, except spades, is in the old 1947 NACA Report 868 and spades have been around since the 1950's.

We weighed those wing root fairings that were removed from the prototype and they were very heavy. We weighed the aeroplane after we recovered it and took out weight and it was still heavier than the official weight in the logbook when the airplane came to us.

I did some in-flight wing tufting to investigate the buffeting experienced when pulling G. We discovered a major source of disturbance was one of the big scoops under the cowl so that was tidied up. It was significantly improved but I didn't explore much after that (I had other work to do) and Mark Heiner did a lot of the test flying. I spent much time trying to improve the engine oil cooling. We didn't get to explore the full envelope before Robert Armstrong took it away.

Robert Armstrong encountered aeroelastic issues with the wing and aileron so Leon Tolve became involved to sort it out.

I left the factory before any more were built. Two were flown successfully with the Black Hawk formation aerobatic team comprising Matt Morrissey and Tom Womack.

If you obtain plans from Aviat you will get the original Super Stinker design with quite a few gaps if you intend to finish with an S-1-11B. Two have since been built in Australia – the first for Chris Sperou which was built locally. Chris is a real inspiration having won the Australian National Championships thirteen times and now aged over 80 he is still doing his energetic low level aerobatic displays including five snap rolls at the top of a loop.

The September 1995 issue of the AOPA Pilot magazine included an article on the Husky by Alton K. Marsh. The article had a photograph of the half-finished prototype of the aerobatic Husky and noted that it "had shorter wings to increase the roll rate" and that there was "debate over whether to install flaps." After the S-1-11B left it was time to address this aerobatic Husky. I found a few aspects of the design which were not suitable, or even viable, and some of these explain why the project had previously stalled.

The Husky trim system using springs provided quite a high stick force gradient with change in airspeed so that needed some redesign for the aerobatic variant. The flap system allowed the flaps to move down under any load in that direction so obviously unsuitable for flight under negative G. Would we change the flap mechanism or remove the flaps? I did some calculations of roll rate. My predecessor had reduced the wingspan but also reduced the aileron span so the outcome was a slower roll rate than the standard Husky and that wasn't going to impress any aerobatic pilot. The wing structural design at that stage was inadequate for the aerobatic category of + 6 G so there was much work to be done.

I decided to reduce the wingspan even further, remove the flaps entirely and retain the standard Husky ailerons. The result was a significant increase in roll rate which was acceptable. We also now had a reduced wing bending moment and our wing spar design was strong enough to take the 6 G now.

Sitting back and looking at what we had I wondered how the market would take it. It seemed to me that it offered no competitive advantage over the Super Decathlon so I wouldn't expect us to make much of an inroad into that market. I recommended to the boss that we drop the idea of an aerobatic Husky and put our efforts into developing the basic Husky. So that is what we did with much more work for us to do on that project.

The Pitts S-2B had been in continuous production for 12 years with nearly 200 having been built in that time but there had been absolutely no design improvements. The fuel gauge was a simple sight tube made from transparent hose routed a long distance from the main tank and, because of the tail down attitude, it was grossly misleading when on the ground. The fresh air vents of the S-2A were removed with the S-2B, that may have been fine in Wyoming but in a hot climate it would become unbearable in the cockpit. The structure was essentially the lighter S-2A with a heavier, more powerful engine and the wings moved to get the CG in the right place. Movement of the wings resulted in a different relative position of the upper and lower wings which changed its snap roll characteristics and not for the better. Now that the canopy was closer to the top wing the slider had a shorter movement so there became more unintentional canopy departures in flight. With its origins in the S-2A structure and the limited increase in maximum weight available for the S-2B, its useful load was less than the S-2A.

Its maximum weight was 1700 lb with aerobatics limited to 1625 lb. The AFM states a "standard empty weight" of 1150 lb but a more typical empty weight would be 1200 lb. Add the engine oil and unusable fuel to that. It leaves a maximum of 425 lb for crew and fuel when doing aerobatics. If loaded with two average young people and half fuel it was within the allowable weight and balance for aerobatics. Take a larger person such as myself and add the weight of parachutes it becomes very easy to load it over the maximum weight and behind the aft CG limit.

The S-2C was to address the above issues plus get away from the classic rounded tail and wingtip with straightening of the underbelly to improve the competition scoring prospects. We got a little way along the track with the 50th Anniversary Pitts that we took to Oshkosh in 1996. It had the strengthened fuselage truss of the S-2C and other refinements which still feature in current production model S-2C aircraft. It got my larger ailerons and attention to the wing design to improve the snap roll characteristics. The fin and rudder were pretty much the same as the one I had earlier sketched up for Sean Tucker.

In 1997 I had two other exciting opportunities – one with another, bigger aircraft manufacturer in the USA and the other as Chief Engineer at the Boeing plant back home in Melbourne, Australia. My family said that they only wanted to move once more in their life so the choice was back to Australia. Nick Guida had previously joined Aviat to bolster the engineering effort and he undertook much of the remaining engineering effort on the S-2C. Eddie Saurenman joined the company after my departure.

Of course, I must recognise the sterling efforts of Lanny Swensen who worked at the Pitts and Husky factory at Afton for very many years. Lanny excelled at CAD design, production tooling design, production troubleshooting and customer service. None of us could have done it without Lanny.

Unfortunately, there is insufficient space to single out any of my other friends at the factory however I still remember them all.

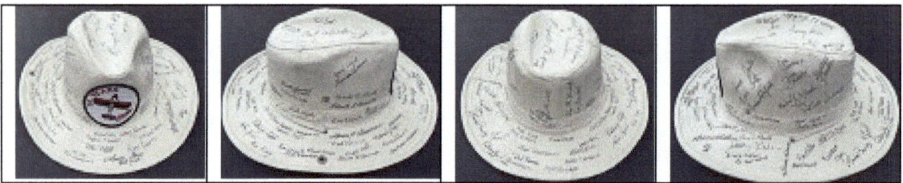

Following a trip to Oshkosh in 2018 I took an interest in the conceptual design of a new model Pitts, tentatively named the S-2X. Michael Stalls developed this initial CAD model. As you can see from my red mark-ups in the diagram below we still have a long way to go with the design.

It is bigger than an S-2C to provide a more comfortable cockpit for two. Nominal specifications for the conceptual design are:

	S-2C	S-2X
LENGTH (ft in)	17' 9"	18' 9"
WINGSPAN (ft in)	20	23' 6"
AEROBATIC FUEL (USG)	23	23
FERRY FUEL TANK (USG)	5	35

BAGGAGE (LB)	20	30
WING AREA (SQ FT)	125	155
EMPTY WEIGHT (LB)	1150	1350
AEROBATIC WEIGHT (LB)	1700	1950
MAXIMUM WEIGHT (LB)	1700	2100
LIMIT LOAD FACTORS	+6/-5	+7/-5
WING LOADING (LB/SQ FT)	13.6	13.5
ENGINE	Lyc AEIO-540-D4A5	Lyc AEIO-580
POWER (HP)	260	315
AERO POWER LOADING (LB/HP)	6.5	6.2
STALL SPEED (KTS)	53	52
CRUISE SPEED (KTS)	150	160
RATE OF CLIMB (FT/MIN)	2100	2300
NEVER EXCEED SPEED (KTS)	184	200

It features composite wing structure rather than the traditional wood and fabric so truly a modern biplane.

3 PITTS CHECKOUT

Having made the decision, the next step is to do it. You will need dual training! With very few exceptions, the Pitts is not the type of airplane that pilots can just jump in and fly safely.

Your own situation will determine your best training solution. Renting, well, lucky you if you can find a Pitts nearby to rent, it becomes a straightforward decision on where to undertake the training. If you have bought a two seat Pitts then it should be easy to find a suitable instructor who would be happy to teach you in your own airplane.

If you have bought a single seat Pitts then you'll need an instructor who has a two seat Pitts available which limits the options. An important further consideration is the transition from the two seater so I will address that later.

Budd Davisson knows more about checking pilots out in a Pitts than anyone else on the planet so he is #1 recommendation for an instructor. However not everyone has the option of visiting him in Arizona but we can all benefit from his knowledge through his books and magazine articles. Check them out at http://www.airbum.com/pitts.html. Some of his comments are so good that I feel obliged to repeat them here from his article in the May 2020 issue of Sport Aerobatics magazine:

"For almost everyone, the first flight in a Pitts is the very definition of sensory overload. ... There are no airplanes normally available to pilots that prepare them for what they're about to experience in terms of rapidity and new surroundings."

"So, is the Pitts a difficult airplane to land? It depends on how you define 'difficult'. I'd say that it is demanding ..."

With over 7,000 hours teaching Pitts landings, Budd certainly knows what he is talking about.

I have done many checkouts in Pitts over the years and have followed the nominal flight training syllabus described in this chapter. If anyone asks, I tell people that it takes ten hours although it is usually shorter than that but it does filter out a lot of pilots who are not committed to it. Most of my training has been in the S-2A but here I will describe the flight training as I do it in the S-2C.

I might recommend a few circuits in the back seat of a Decathlon if one is readily available as it gives you an idea of the limited visibility from a Pitts but doesn't really help the training. It does mean that Decathlon instructors feel more comfortable, at first, in the Pitts as they are already familiar with not seeing anything out the front.

I know that some instructors start their trainees out in the front seat. Life is more simple in the front seat but the sight picture is different so then you would need to transition to the rear seat. Extra tasks in the back seat are starting and stopping the engine, in-flight engine/system management, elevator trim and the radio controls. If I felt that I needed to start a trainee in the front seat then I would have made the decision that this is just a "joy-flight" and the pilot is not ready to commence a Pitts checkout - stay with the Decathlon!

Seating position and eye height is important. Use cushions if necessary, firm foam pads are better than soft cushions. Allow adequate clearance between the top of your helmet or headset that you won't scratch the canopy in negative G manoeuvres. The higher you are the more you will be able to see!

Your first flight in a Pitts should be some general familiarisation flying to get to know it, including some basic aerobatics. Pilots typically come from something like the Super Decathlon with basic spin and aerobatic training under their belt and therefore some tailwheel experience. Even in basic aerobatics it does things quite differently.

For aerobatics in the Pitts S-2A I use a power setting of 2500 RPM and 25" MP so expect a fuel burn rate of about 18 US Gall/hr or about 70 litres/hr. In the Pitts S-2C expect 25 US Gall/hr or 95 litres/hr.

With two up you probably won't be taking full fuel so it is particularly important to decide in advance the fuel level at which you will return to base. Use the fuel flow meter with totalizer as it is quite accurate if set up correctly. Cowl flap as required but expect perhaps 2/3 closed.

You will quickly learn that the Pitts is an extremely docile airplane with the power off. Power off stalls are characterised by the normal nose down pitch and perhaps a slight uncommanded roll, the latter depending a lot on the wing rigging. Stalls with full throttle are also quite benign as you would have the aeroplane fairly well balanced. Stall recovery is a non-event and, anyway, I ensure that my trainees are very competent in the basics before starting in the Pitts, otherwise back to the Super Decathlon.

Having mentioned wing rigging it is worthwhile discussing this in some detail here. I recall one new production Pitts S-2B which Peter Pierpont, Chief Test Pilot at Aviat at the time, wanted me to test fly as he said that its recovery from a one turn spin wasn't normal despite several attempts at rigging it. I looked at what had been done with the rigging and the outcome. It was one of those where they had gone around the rigging process and got to where it was at the limit of the number of washers under the I-struts. It seemed OK so we prepared to go flying. Peter decided to ride along in the front seat although I, as an FAA approved production test pilot, was authorised to do it and sign it off if appropriate. The avionics were to be fitted after it had gained its CofA so I had a portable radio strapped to one knee and a portable intercom on the other knee. Both of us were wearing parachutes and helmets. With a ground elevation of 6,000 ft the pre-flight briefing included the statement that in the event that recovery was not occurring by 9,000 ft then I would call "bail-out" three times and I would not be in the aeroplane on the third call. I started with a straight stall then a one turn spin in each direction. All seemed normal so then I climbed back up to 12,000 ft to initiate a three-turn spin to the right. At three turns I initiated the normal recovery controls however my right arm was caught on the intercom box, just enough that recovery was being delayed. I knew what was happening so wasn't concerned however it took me a little bit of time to correct the problem and recover the spin. On the other hand, Peter in the front seat was unaware of what was really happening. All he knew was that we had gone way beyond three turns with no sign of a recovery so was expecting the "bail-out" command very soon.

When I arrived at Aviat I had not previously flown the B model Pitts nor the Husky so I was given very thorough check-outs by Greg Poe as he was filling the test pilot's role at the time. One flight was focused on spinning and we exercised every spin mode including inverted flat spins in both directions. His entry to inverted spins was from 160 mph then pull up to a climb of about 45° then hit the controls for a neat dynamic entry saves hanging from the straps inverted for a long time, he said. At the end of it Greg asked if I wanted to see his new party trick. Nope, I'd had enough of being tumbled around but I did offer to fly it myself if he just gave me some directions on how to do it. Nope, he wasn't going to let me try a double hammerhead.

The thing about Greg and I in an S-2B with parachutes and quite a bit of fuel was that we were above the maximum aerobatic weight and behind the aft CG limit. I discussed this with others too and they also had undertaken extensive spinning in this configuration with no problems. Unfortunately, we didn't have a spin test report and the other test data necessary to extend the CG envelope. So, we knew that it could be done safely but we certainly had no idea where the real limit might be. In spinning, with the complex solution of aerodynamic and inertia forces and moments representing the small difference between large numbers it is common to encounter cliff-edge effects. i.e. take a step, all good, take another step and still good, then another step and still no adverse change in the behaviour but take one further small step and everything suddenly turns bad. The point is – remain within the allowable weight and balance range otherwise you become a test pilot.

As with stalls, the Super Decathlon pilot would be very familiar with side-slipping approaches to land so a short revision should suffice.

Rolls! I'll never forget Brad Mulcahy complaining to me after his first flight in a Pitts. He said if he had known how well it rolled, how fast and how easy then he would've transitioned from the Decathlon much earlier. Just pick a reference point ahead and move the stick to the side. A slight forward nudge on the stick as it goes inverted with slight foot movements on the rudder pedals results in a very neat slow roll. So easy! Not much more need be said about rolls at this stage except to relate a few experiences.

I took the factory demonstrator to the University of North Dakota and flew with three of their instructors and a senior airline pilot who was visiting. All the instructors were excellent pilots as, after I demonstrated a landing, they all did a good landing themselves. There are three flights that I will never forget. I was especially impressed with one who had previously been a Russian fighter pilot as I had him doing vertically upward snap rolls in that short flight. One did some gentle barrel and aileron rolls then asked if he could use full aileron deflection. Back then I used to claim that the S-2B would roll at 240 deg/sec which I thought would be double the rate of the Super Decathlon they were using. I see now from the Facebook Roll Challenge that a Super Decathlon actually rolls at about 90 deg/sec and the S-2B at about 150 deg/sec. Incidentally, I see a Cessna Aerobat there at 60 deg/sec and the S-2C at 205 deg/sec. He certainly gave it full aileron but also used the Decathlon technique with equivalent forward pressure on the stick. Headsets flew all around the cockpit! Debriefing after landing he asked what would happen now as we had gone to -5 G which was far beyond the limit load factor of -3 G. I simply replied that I would retain that setting on the accelerometer to show everyone else how strong the aeroplane was. As factory Chief Engineer I knew where the structural margins were and where there weren't any. We knew that repeated snap rolls at higher than recommended airspeeds would cause fatigue cracking in fuselage longerons and failure if not detected in maintenance inspections.

Then my own experience flying with Bill Finagin in his Pitts S-2C in 2008 at a time when I had done a lot of Decathlon flying but hadn't flown a Pitts for many years. I could fly it fine he said except that I was rolling it like a Decathlon, not a Pitts!

When you learnt loops in a Cessna Aerobat or Super Decathlon, for example, you would discover that the right entry speed and a decent initial pull back on the stick followed by a slight relaxation going over the top would produce a passable loop. They would go around so easily and nothing much would go wrong. The technique is similar in the Pitts. The recommended entry speed is in the range 130 to 180 mph. Our S-2C has an ASI with both mph and kts with mph on the outer ring so more prominent and therefore my choice of units. Don't mix them up! If there is any excessive back pressure at the top of a loop the Pitts will positively stall with an uncommanded roll. Easily recovered but will result in the loop being aborted if actions are not prompt.

My experience is that the S-2A is more docile in this situation and can be coaxed to continue while in the stall buffet. After my own checkout in an S-2A I started flying the S-1C. This only had two ailerons so didn't roll as fast but it had much greater performance to more than make up for it. Unlike the S-2A it had "flat-bottomed" wings so was a delight to loop with positive G. The aircraft was owned by a club and we decided to build a set of S-1S wings with four ailerons for it. Would you believe that not one of us could complete a normal loop in it! Every time we got to the top it would do a complete snap roll. Oh well, good incentive to move up a category so that we fly more complex figures without having to do a normal loop.

Hammerheads are where new Pitts pilots really learn how the power effects and gyroscopic propeller forces influence the behaviour of high performance aerobatic aircraft. As with the Super Decathlon it is important to get a good vertical on the up line. Use the controls as necessary to keep it straight and don't hit the rudder too early. Wait …. wait ….. There are different cues available to you.

A tuft of yarn on the sighting device is my personal choice – when the end of it starts to flicker then it is time to go. If the yarn turns around and points forward then it means you are flying backwards – that's OK as there is plenty of propeller slipstream over the tail for you to  continue and fly. You should get this Pitts sighting device, designed by Bill Finagin, from Aviat as it is essential for accurate aerobatic flying.

Another cue is the aileron deflection. If you are flying a good vertical line then as the airspeed approaches zero you will be giving it quite a bit of stick to the right. When you see the aileron at about half deflection then it is time to hit the rudder.

David Hooke, the pilot in the photograph above, undertook some Pitts aerobatic training at Tutima Academy of Aviation Safety which he recommends highly. His instructor told him to wait until the ASI needle was down to the "H" in the "MPH" at the top of the instrument in small print. It works well but note that when sitting on the ground the needle should be centred on the "P" so you are almost stopped.

Hit the rudder firmly, briskly and hold it. At the same time you are going to need lots more aileron and a lot of forward stick to maintain the plane of rotation in yaw.

We're only going to do them to the left in the S-2C. In the Super Decathlon I require my aerobatic students to do them both left and right but with a Pitts the power effects overwhelm the aerodynamics at slow speed. You can do hammerheads to the right by reducing power but you're really not going to encounter a need to do it.

If you don't use the correct hammerhead technique, especially if you hit the left rudder too early and apply full forward stick with full right aileron you have a lot of excess energy which the airplane will use to aggressively go to a negative stall and directly into an inverted flat spin. After all, that is what you have commanded by those control inputs. Get that advanced spin training described in Chapter 5.

Both knowledge and skills are required in a Pitts checkout in appropriate doses as they are in most aspects of aviation training. In these chapters on the checkout, I don't intend to duplicate information in the aircraft manuals nor briefings to be provided by your flight instructor. The S-2C AFM is very comprehensive and I will highlight some important points and indicate how to use some of the information. I recommend that trainees go through CASA's single engine aircraft endorsement questionnaire and answer all of the relevant questions to learn about the airplane prior to commencing flight training. Read the whole AFM as well. In Chapter 4 I go through the questionnaire in some detail for the S-2A.

Your first pre-flight inspection guided by your flight instructor will teach you much about the airplane. The AFM has a comprehensive checklist but there is little detail on exactly what to look for with some of the items so pay attention to your instructor. Pay particular attention to inspection for FOD inside the cockpit and remove the rear seat back to check inside the rear fuselage.

Your flight instructor will demonstrate the first takeoff with you following his actions lightly on the controls. The Hartzell Claw propeller has three big blades with a large diameter of 78" so I like to keep the tail slightly low, especially on grass. The S-2C AFM has good guidance with airspeed numbers and technique so do it per the book. 100 mph for the initial climb after takeoff then 120 mph for a cruise climb at 2400 RPM and 23" MP.

Taking control after takeoff you will notice the extra attention needed on the rudder to keep the aircraft in balance during the climb.

Your flight instructor will also demonstrate the first approach and landing. Depending on how busy your airfield is you will either be doing a tight base to final or a more normal base further away from the runway with a straight sideslip to keep the runway in sight on final. Even with the tight base style you may find it useful to allow a short straight final to assist in lining up the runway and checking what I call the gate prior to continuing for a landing. A continuous turn to the runway, straightening up as the flare is commenced is also a suitable technique. Your flight instructor will brief you for your lessons.

Fly the downwind leg at a slow cruise speed, say 2400 RPM and about 15" MP. Trim the elevator.

Turn onto base and reduce power, even close the throttle, but note that the S-2C with that big Claw propeller will readily lose airspeed if an appropriate descent rate is not achieved. I recommend an airspeed of 105 mph for my trainees. I find that new, young especially, pilot trainees want to know a number whenever I say reduce power. If we are not going to close the throttle on base then here is a number for you: 1800 RPM. In reality, reduce it enough – enough to maintain the airspeed and get to the runway from where we are.

Fly it at 105 mph and trim to keep it steady. It doesn't take much lack of attention to find yourself in a situation where you are undershooting and the airspeed is rapidly decaying. Be ready to add power as required.

At the gate, just before crossing the fence, verify that the airspeed is 100

– 105 mph and steady, the power is steady and the aircraft is lined up on the centre-line of the runway. If the gate is not achieved then go round!

If the gate is achieved then slowly reduce power and, at about hangar height you will find that the airspeed will be back at 95 mph (the book figure) but there is no need to concern yourself with airspeed at this point.

Gently start the flare and aim to level off close to the ground, in the three point attitude – then hold the stick steady. That last word is important! The controls are extremely powerful so don't use any more than necessary and don't suddenly make large control inputs.  Any error in attitude, make it slightly tail first. In fact, the AFM states that "landing should be made on the tail wheel first to reduce the landing speed and subsequent need for braking"!

With the airplane straight it is important to look straight ahead. Become familiar with the sight picture of the ground either side of the nose.

Use peripheral vision rather than looking just to one side.

Once you have the correct attitude just above the ground with zero descent rate then hold the stick steady. It is that simple. Slowly easing the stick further back as you would during the landing flare in a Decathlon won't work in the Pitts – it will cause a balloon. Hold the stick firmly such that it doesn't bounce around at touchdown.

Once on the ground, slowly ease the stick back and before long you will be taxiing. It is going fast when touching down compared to other types you have flown up until now so keep on your toes and keep it straight. As airspeed reduces during a landing on a sealed runway the classic directional instability of a tailwheel airplane will be evident. Keep the stick back and steer with rudder.

Don't be afraid to use full rudder in either direction but never hold it more than an instant. Keep your toes away from the brakes but if you really need the brakes to avoid a ground loop then use them. Better to have fixed it earlier however and even gone around for another landing.

Use your peripheral vision all throughout the landing. When at a slow taxi speed you can revert to the zig-zag taxi, looking out each side in turn.

The words I use in briefing and in flight are similar to those I use in the

Super Decathlon but it responds very much quicker. As Budd said, "it is demanding".

The AFM states that "wheel landings are approved". Fine, but I'm going to limit my typical trainee to many hours of just three-point landings before I will even discuss this subject. Facebook with Spencer Suderman and the others provide much entertaining discussion on this subject.

Advanced spin training is essential. The S-2C AFM states "All spins are approved in the Aerobatic Category. We strongly recommend getting the appropriate spin training before any aerobatic flight in the Pitts. Any aerobatic maneuver if done incorrectly can become a spin." Excellent advice and exactly what I have been saying since I commenced giving aerobatic instruction in an S-2A in 1980.

The Pitts checkout largely comprises circuit work. On a quiet airfield I would generally do landings to a full stop then taxi back for another takeoff. This allows the complete landing to be exercised with time for a thorough debrief prior to the next takeoff and circuit.

Emergency procedures are included as usual. A landing without engine power is not a lot different from the normal landings that I have already described. If you are operating at a busy Class D airfield however you will have to specifically include these exercises in the syllabus. A simulated engine failure after takeoff should also be included in the training.

Transitioning to a single seat Pitts is a consideration for many pilots. After completing your checkout in the two-seater as above then get your instructor to sit in the back while you do a few circuits in the front seat. You will find that the sight picture is like the S-1. Nothing will prepare you for the extra performance and nimble controls, however. The feeling of going from the Super Decathlon to the S-2 is repeated when you go from the S-2 to the S-1.

As with flying in general and tailwheel airplanes in particular, it is even more important to keep current in the Pitts. If I haven't flown a Pitts for some time I like to grab another instructor to come with me for a quick circuit. It is easy to become just that slight bit rusty such that you are a little bit off with judgement and feel which can make things turn out bad for you.

What equipment do you need as a Pitts pilot?

CASA made these recommendations for airline passengers so this a good start for all pilots. "In the improbable event of an emergency, the clothes you are wearing can play a significant role in your safety. People wear synthetic blend fabrics …. However, they ignite quickly, shrink, melt, and continue burning after the heat source is removed.
…..

Wearing clothes made of natural fibres such as cotton, wool, denim and leather offer the best protection during an evacuation or fire.
….

Avoid leaving large areas of the body uncovered. …. Wear non-restrictive clothing as this allows you greater movement.
….

The most common injuries to feet during accidents or emergencies can be prevented by wearing suitable footwear. Wearing fully enclosed leather low-heeled laced or buckled shoes, boots or tennis shoes is recommended."

There are additional considerations in flying a Pitts. The cockpit is open to the fuselage interior and control runs so it is important not to drop small items in flight. This includes mobile phones as they will invariably end up at the tail of the aeroplane with the risk of jamming the elevator. A flight suit will keep your essential items safely zipped but accessible if needed during the flight. It will also be made from a fire-resistant material, usually Nomex. Pilots these days seem to be more fashion conscious than I was when younger so have a look around at what others are wearing and why. My recent choice was black to assist with air-to-air photography however it is not the best choice under a bubble canopy on a hot day.

The rear seat of a Pitts S-2B or S-2C has a narrow tunnel for your lower legs and feet on the pedals. The A models are open to the front cockpit so the person on the front seat can interfere with your pedal movement. Thin shoes are essential. The soles of shoes must be smooth so as not to grab on the floor or pedals which would result in notchy movement. Bicycle and Go-Kart shoes work well. I like my new LIFT pilot shoes with the patented "rudder control heel slider". May as well look the part!

I often wear flying gloves even if only to keep my hands away from grime accumulated on the control stick of a forty-year-old airplane. They are certainly a good safety item in the event of fire.

A Pitts cockpit is tight with a lot of hard objects close to your head. If you suffer an engine failure and a subsequent forced landing, then consider the risk of head injury in landing rough at about 95 mph. My choice of helmet is the Bonehead PilotX although there are many others to choose from.

David Pilkington
Bruno Roque & David Hooke

Parachutes are the final items to discuss here. Some countries, notably the USA, mandate them in some aerobatic operations so the flight school would make them available. The International Aerobatic Club requires them for contests in the USA. Parachutes are not required for Australian powered aircraft aerobatics however some flight schools choose to provide them in training. Serious competition aerobatic pilots wear them as a matter of course. Personally, I recommend parachutes in advanced spin training and in advanced aerobatic competition and practice.

If you do wear a parachute make sure that you maintain an appropriate discipline of operating with it. First, get some basic instruction in the care and use of it as well as the operational procedure. John Morrisey explained the importance of this in his article, 23 Seconds, in the May 2016 issue of Sport Aerobatics magazine. "If the spin is entered from 3,500 feet and cannot be stopped at the desired number of rotations, for whatever reason, bailing out is no longer a viable option to save the pilot. There is no longer enough time or altitude to exit the plane and open the chute."

His trials demonstrated that it would take 23 seconds from the onset of an unexpected bailout situation to exit his airplane, a Pitts S-2S. Egress from the bubble canopy of other S-2 models would be quicker with its canopy jettisoning system. In dual training operations you must identify a bail-out altitude or "hard deck" at which you will brief the mandatory action of bailing out if the aircraft is not under control. In determining that height you must consider the manoeuvres at risk and something like that 23 seconds to escape the cockpit and still be high enough for the parachute to be effective.

In normal training operations you then must remain far enough above that hard deck that you are not unnecessarily jumping out of perfectly good airplane or, perhaps worse, ignoring the hard deck.

Allen Silver's website http://silverparachutes.com/ has his excellent seminar handouts, Emergency Bailout Procedures and Survival Equipment for Pilots, freely available.

4 ENDORSEMENT QUESTIONNAIRE

CASA has a template for a single engine aircraft endorsement questionnaire which is useful as the basis for the knowledge assessment by a flight instructor. It is even more useful for the pilot as it obliges you to go through the manuals looking for useful information. I tell all of my trainees to complete this questionnaire before they commence flight training as it will save them money. It doesn't cost anything to read the manuals and sit in the aeroplane just familiarising yourself with the instruments and controls! With very few exceptions, few bother to do it, instead they want their instructor to tell them what they need to know. Not with me however, if you don't want to read the Flight Manual then go elsewhere.

The questionnaire notes "The document will serve as a ready reference for you in the future, particularly if you do not fly regularly." Good advice.

I assume that my trainees have read the Flight Manual and ideally have completed this questionnaire before we start the flight training. Note that this chapter follows the one about the flight training for the Pitts checkout as that is what normally happens unfortunately. I seem to be chasing pilots to complete the questionnaire before sending them solo.

I start each flight lesson with a thorough pre-flight briefing and the first flight is even more thorough. The final part of that first pre-flight briefing is done with the trainee seated in the cockpit to ensure that he (a verbal embrace) is familiar with all the actions and observations required during the flight. By then the pilot would've already gone through the checklist items and is expected to know much of it already so this should be a revision and review.

Let's go through the parts of that questionnaire to hit the highlights for the Pitts S-2A. Why the S-2A when I am explaining the checkout in an S-2C? Two reasons: the first is that I don't want to spoon feed you – go through the questionnaire yourself and learn about the airplane. Secondly, there is some additional information available for the S-2A which will help all pilots at this stage.

Section 2 identifies all the airspeed limitations and some of the key airspeeds for operating the airplane. G limitations are covered too. The interesting thing about the S-2A AFM is that most airspeeds are specified in CAS rather than IAS as required by FAR 23 at the time. For example, maneuvering speed is stated as 134 kts CAS whereas the old Australian AFM for the type states 130 kts. V_{NE} is 176 kts CAS or 172 kts IAS. Obviously, the ASI is displaying speeds in IAS so that is what the pilot needs to know. The airspeed indicator should have markings in CAS as required by its certification. Unless you convert to IAS you are at a high risk of exceeding V_{NE} or exceeding the limitations associated with V_A! However, pilots are not provided with the conversion between CAS and IAS so they are unaware of this issue.

The S-2A is one of the few types which makes the structural flight envelope available in the Owner's and Maintenance Manual. S-2A pilots should seek this document as it is much useful information in it. You will be unable to complete this questionnaire without it. It includes this useful text:

"This means, in practical language, that at indicated airspeeds of 154 mph or less, you may apply sudden full aileron, rudder, or nose-up elevator deflection without exceeding the airframe minimum design loads. Sudden full nose-down elevator may likewise be applied at 106 mph indicated or less, without exceeding the design loads."

I refer the reader to Aerobatics Down Under for general guidance on the use of controls above V_A.

The AFM states that the flight load factors are + 6.0 G and -3.0 G however the V-G diagram provided here clearly shows that the negative G limit reduces above 126 kts by so much that only -1.5 G is permitted at V_{NE}. Don't be lulled into thinking this is just a paperwork number to be ignored as, even though the wing may be strong enough to withstand -3.0 G it is likely that this corner of the flight envelope is the critical design case for the horizontal tail. This cut-off in the negative load factor at high speeds is a feature of FAR 23 so it probably applies to almost all airplanes. Is it applicable to the Pitts S-2C that we will be flying?

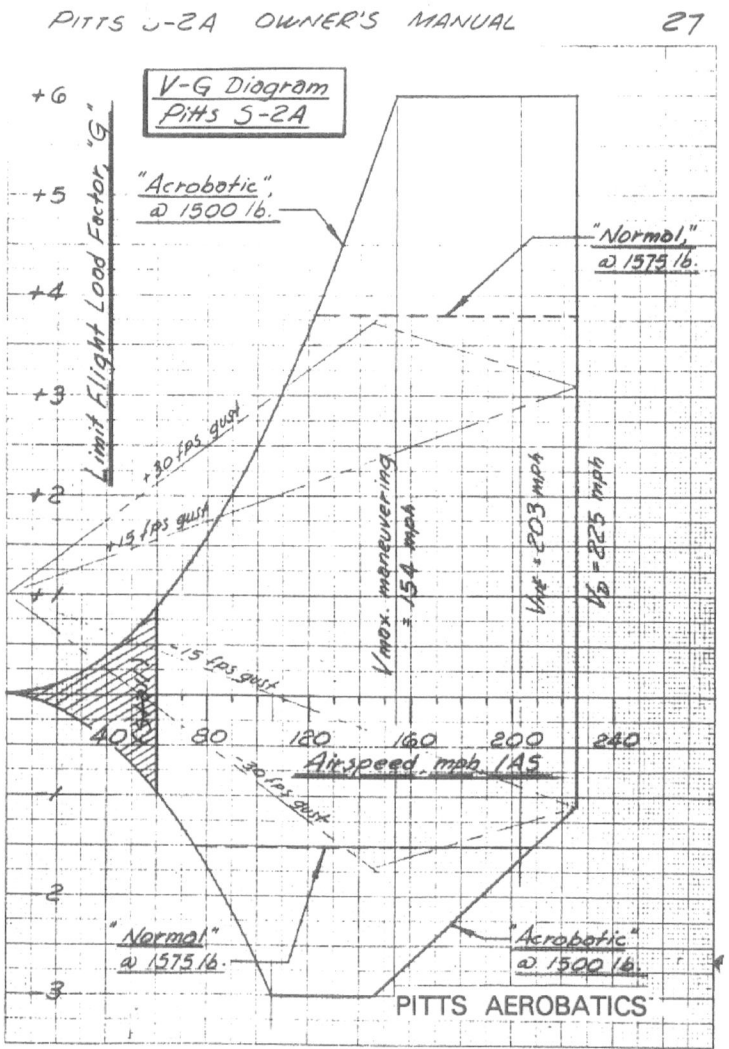

The document goes on to state: "If you now compare the recommended entry speeds for various demonstrated maneuvers, shown on this page, with the V-G diagram, it should be clear that if you feel you need more airspeed than the tabulated values show, you are not properly performing the maneuver, and you may be overloading the airframe. Do not exceed the limitations shown on the V-G diagram; every maneuver in the Aresti ladder can be performed from combinations of the ones shown here." More good advice!

APPROVED MANEUVERS AND RECOMMENDED ENTRY SPEEDS:(MPH)

MANEUVER	INSIDE MAX.	INSIDE MIN.	OUTSIDE MAX.	OUTSIDE MIN.
LOOP (UP)	180	130	180	130
LOOP (DOWN)	100	70	100	70
SLOW ROLL	180	100	180	100
BARREL ROLL	180	130	180	130
SNAP ROLL	140	90	110	90
HAMMERHEAD	180	130	180	130
LAZY EIGHT	180	140	180	140
CHANDELLE	180	140	180	140
STALLS AND SPINS	(SLOW DECELERATION)			

I have this theory that pilots never read placards and I test this out when I'm flying with trainees in the Super Decathlon. After my guidance to read the manuals, I am always amazed when pilots are unable to operate the park brake correctly, especially as the instructions are on a placard adjacent to the park brake knob.

This placard on maneuver entry speeds may not have to be referenced in flight but pilots must be familiar with it. Particularly important is the range of recommended speeds for snap rolls – 78 kts to 122 kts. I regard the upper end of that range as a limitation rather than a recommendation. I had the opportunity to conduct some snap rolls in an S-2B with on-board recording instrumentation of strain gauges. At 122 kts I was doing 6 G in a snap roll which is the maximum positive flight limit load factor but what about the rolling G limit?

Section 3 covers all the emergency procedures. You generally don't get time to read the AFM in an emergency and, even if you did, where is it in the S-2A? Inaccessible in the luggage compartment behind the pilot however most S-2C examples have it handy in a pouch beside the pilot's elbow. Engine fire on the ground, engine fire airborne, engine failure after take-off and so on. Trainees must know the relevant emergency procedures.

Section 4 goes through some of the normal procedures. One of the questions is to obtain the cruise performance at 65% power at 5,000 ft altitude and then calculate the endurance. For the S-2A we see that 2400 RPM at 65% power gives a TAS of 140 mph or 122 kts. The charts show a fuel burn of 9.1 USG/hr or 34.6 litres/hr. What MP do we need to get 65% power and that fuel flow? If you don't get the power setting correct then the manual's guidance on fuel flow will be useless and your flight planning will be hit and miss. You need to do better than that to safely operate the Pitts with its limited endurance. My own notes from an old set of S-2A handling notes show a MP of 23 in.Hg which works quite well at very low altitudes with 22 in.Hg being more appropriate at around 4,000 ft. This is one reason for pilots to read the Lycoming Operator's Manual for the Aerobatic Engines. Spend a little time familiarizing yourself with the performance charts and develop your own table of power settings at different altitudes.

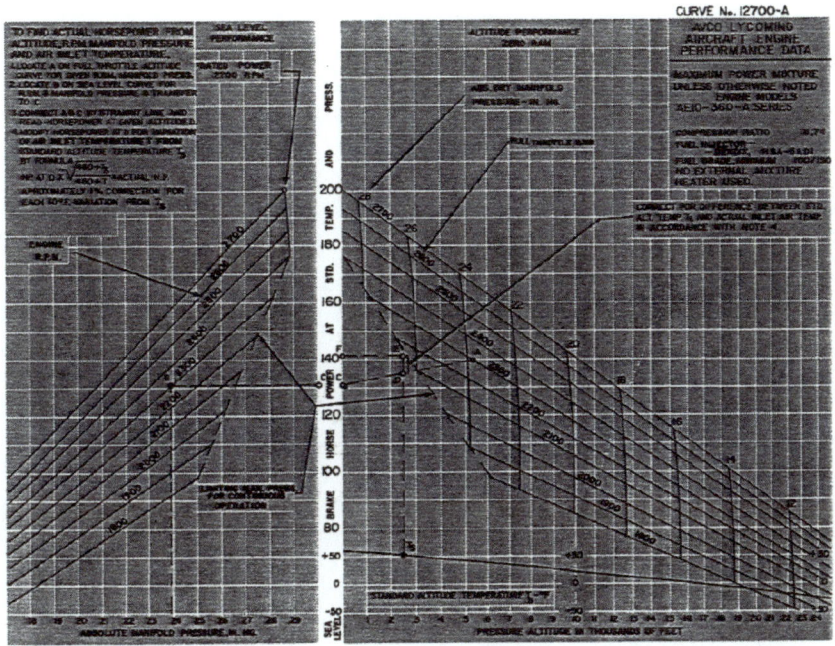

Figure 4-4. Sea Level and Altitude Performance - AEIO-360-A Series

It is extremely important to properly lean the engine. If your S-2A only has the standard factory instrumentation then you have scant information to rely on so be conservative and build up some knowledge from actual flight observations. The fuel pressure gauge is calibrated to show fuel flow however the scale is very small at that power setting. The fuel gauge itself in the S-2A is accurate but vague. Indicators are simple, only at quarters of the tank, to make it very challenging to keep an

accurate fuel log.

My experience is that you will achieve that performance with the double bubble canopy but not with open cockpits.

With 23 USG or 87.4 litres of useable fuel the endurance is only 2 hrs 30 mins. In practical cross-country flight planning you will obviously need to allow for the usual taxi, takeoff and climb fuel as well as forecast winds. Remember that there must be a good allowance for the time spent at high power with mixture rich as it will eat significantly into the fuel before you settle down into the normal cruise. A good rule of thumb is to look for airfields no more than 200 nm apart for refuelling stops. For most people, that is about as long as you would want to spend in the confined cockpit with that upright seat back.

I have seen the sad outcome of one flight with a planned distance of 212 nm into a brisk headwind but which only achieved 211 nm due to poor piloting and bad planning. It resulted in significant damage to the aircraft and the occupants were very lucky to have escaped serious injury.

Section 5 deals with weight and balance plus airfield performance. Like many GA aerobatic aircraft, the useful load is marginal however both the S-2A and the S-2C can be flown reasonably as two seaters. In Australia there is no requirement for parachutes so for these calculations we'll omit them at this stage. I like to see a trainee do weight and balance calculations for a typical aerobatic training flight as well as a cross-country flight. Both reveal important operating limitations. If your Pitts is fitted with a smoke tank that will further reduce the fuel that can be carried.

My experience is that 50% of pilots undertaking a tailwheel endorsement on the Super Decathlon are unable to correctly determine the weight and balance! Hard to believe for such a simple airplane but that includes commercial pilots and flight instructors. The Pitts is also a simple airplane however the loading system in the AFM is a masterpiece eliciting incredulity and confusion when a pilot first unfolds it.

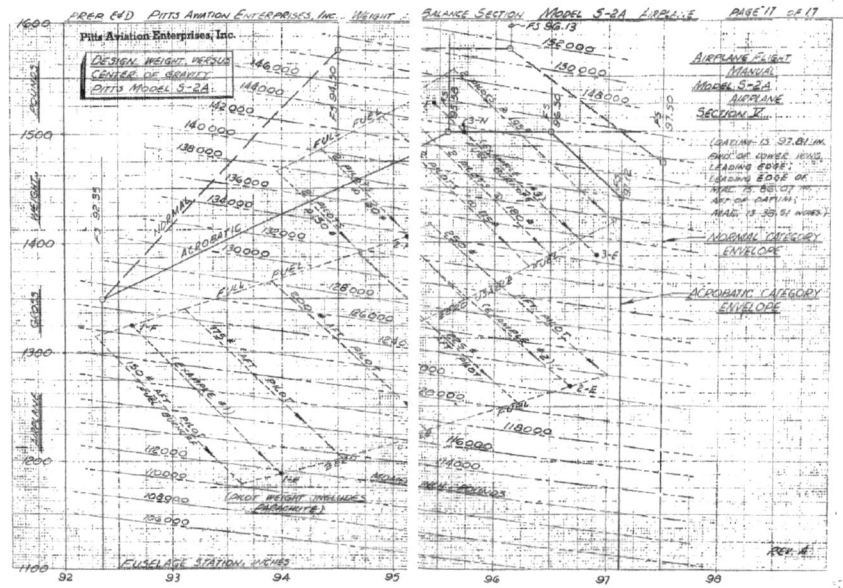

Airfield performance in types certified to early versions of FAR 23 always leads to a good discussion as there was no requirement for take-off and landing distances to be measured and certified for the AFM.

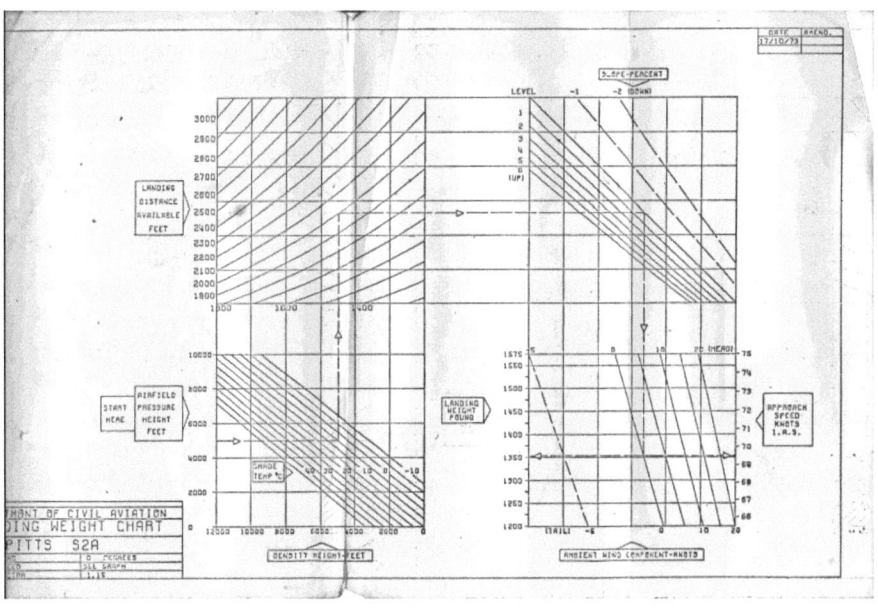

Fortunately, for this book, I have a copy of the old Australian AFM for the S-2A. Back then, the Australian authority at the time would produce their own "P" Charts.

Student pilots in Australia learn about some old CASA standard loading systems for their theory exams and seem incapable of working out real life examples such as the very simple one for the Super Decathlon nor the neat graphical one for the Pitts.

When I worked at Aviat I had the opportunity to be mentored by Herb Andersen who had started at the Call Aircraft Company in 1953 and later became Manager. E.H. "Herb" Andersen became the President and General Manager at Aerotek Inc as the Afton factory transitioned to manufacture of the Pitts S-2A which Curtis Pitts had certified in 1971. Herb was also Chief Engineer and a Designated Engineering Representative, DER, of the FAA. Herb spent much of his life in those roles through different company owners and company names for the Afton factory. Herb had recently retired form full-time work when I arrived at the start of 1995 but he would drop in every week to assist so I enjoyed our many chats. He would accuse me of Australianisms and so on but he soon realized that we almost always ended up with the same engineering view of things. I built up experience there, my Australian engineering authorities standing for nought, and eventually gained my own DER authority – the first Australian to have ever been granted one that I am aware of.

One of the stories that Herb told me was about the S-2A performance charts. When Herb certified the S-2B he wanted to use the existing S-2A performance charts for the AFM to save the expense of conducting takeoff and landing trials. FAR 23 had changed to require additional certified performance data in the AFM and that included the takeoff and landing distances. Afton has an elevation of 6200 ft so the team would have to travel to a lower elevation to conduct a second set of trials as the FAA limits the permissible deviations between test conditions and conditions provided for in the AFM. The FAA sought the test data and report on the analysis supporting the S-2A charts in the Owner's and Maintenance Manual. That data would've been developed by Curtis and his team at Homestead Florida back in 1970 or so. Herb told the FAA that Australia had approved takeoff and landing charts in their Flight Manual but the FAA rejected that as there was nil reporting of the method of data analysis and traceability back to real test data. So, the S-2B was certified in 1983 after having to undergo new flight tests with data analysed by a DER for the FAA approved AFM.

The Australian authority in 1973 simply took the Pitts charts and regurgitated the data into the format of the "P" Charts. So there was some doubling up on the analysis from the original test data by Curtis and it left a gap in the verification of the figures. The analysis of such data is fairly straightforward, but it does result in the extrapolation of results with errors building up the further one goes from the test conditions. The UK CAA's Safety Sense Leaflet 7C, Aeroplane Performance, uses those same analysis methods to provide generic factors to be used in conjunction with FAR 23 AFM airfield distance data. The American charts only give data for a level, sealed runway. The Pitts data is provided at a weight of 1500 lb which is less than the maximum takeoff weight.

FACTORS MUST BE MULTIPLIED e.g. 1.20 x 1.35				
	TAKE-OFF		LANDING	
CONDITION	INCREASE IN TAKE-OFF DISTANCE TO HEIGHT 50 FEET	FACTOR	INCREASE IN LANDING DISTANCE FROM 50 FEET	FACTOR
A 10% increase in aeroplane weight, e.g. another passenger	20%	1.20	10%	1.10
An increase of 1,000 ft in aerodrome elevation	10%	1.10	5%	1.05
An increase of 10°C in ambient temperature	10%	1.10	5%	1.05
Dry grass* - Up to 20 cm (8 in) (on firm soil)	20%	1.20	15%⁺	1.15
Wet grass* - Up to 20 cm (8 in) (on firm soil)	30%	1.3	35%⁺	1.35
			Very short grass may be slippery, distances may increase by up to 60%	
Wet paved surface	-	-	15%	1.15
A 2% slope*	Uphill 10%	1.10	Downhill 10%	1.10
A tailwind component of 10% of lift-off speed	20%	1.20	20%	1.20
Soft ground or snow*	25% or more	1.25 +	25%⁺ or more	1.25 +
NOW USE ADDITIONAL SAFETY FACTORS (if data is unfactored)		1.33		1.43

Notes:
1. * Effect on Ground Run/Roll will be greater. Do not attempt to use the factors to reduce the distances required in the case of downslope on take-off or upslope on landing.
2. ⁺ For a few types of aeroplane (e.g. those without brakes) grass surfaces may decrease the landing roll. However, to be on the safe side, assume the INCREASE shown until you are thoroughly conversant with the aeroplane type.
3. Any deviation from normal operating techniques is likely to result in an increased distance.

If the distance required exceeds the distance available, changes will HAVE to be made.

This CASA questionnaire is intended to relate to practical operation of the aircraft and the sample requires distances at maximum weight, 2500 ft AMSL and an OAT of 30°C on a grass runway. The information in that

Safety Sense Leaflet will get us the data we need to safely operate the Pitts. I also like to recommend the safety factors provided by the UK CAA as the typical pilot is unable to achieve book figures derived from test data.

That Safety Sense Leaflet recommends a 10% increase in takeoff distance and a 5% increase in landing distance for that weight increase. Taking their recommendation for the effects of weight, short dry grass and the safety factors we end up with takeoff and landing distances of 1957 ft (or 597 m) and 2538 ft (or 774 m).

CASA's AC 91-02, Guidelines for aeroplanes with MTOW not exceeding 5700 kg – suitable places to take off and land, also has some useful advice similar to that Safety Sense Leaflet. It has a lower additional safety factor of only 1.15 (up to 2,000 kg) so one should allow additional margins if you cannot nail the airspeed exactly – increase the distance by the speed squared.

Section 6 is about the fuel and oil systems. It is important to note the statement in the manual "Do not perform low altitude aerobatics with less than ¼ tank of fuel on board." The flop tube is unable to scavenge fuel so engine stoppage is likely.

You will have to go to the Lycoming Operator's Manual for the AEIO-360 engine for the source of some of the information required here. It is well worthwhile reading all the section on Operating Instructions to get to know the engine. The aerobatic variants do have some different behaviours as a result of the additional oil lines and different flow paths. Even with the inverted oil system you will see short indications of zero oil pressure and that is normal for some manoeuvres. There is a ten second limitation on flight in the following situations with the risk of engine damage:

- Vertical flight
- Zero G
- Knife-edge

Of course, the behaviour of the oil will depend on the specific layout of the inverted system in your aircraft.

Lycoming states that the minimum safe oil quantity in flight is 4 US qts however you will find improved behaviour of the oil pressure indications with more oil. The Lycoming manual provides good guidance on determining the "normal oil level". You will find that with much more than 6 US qts just one short aerobatic flight will dump a lot of oil and that when down to 6 it will tend to stabilise there. So, only add oil when it gets below 6. If the aircraft is privately owned I recommend just adding ½ US qt but a flight school would be obliged to add the full bottle to save tracking and securing open bottles of oil.

Section 7 is about the engine and propeller details. For those new to constant-speed aerobatic propellers the important question is "If the oil pressure to the dome is lost, does the propeller go into coarse or fine pitch?" Loss of oil pressure after a long vertical down line at high airspeed is the situation to consider. Your propeller better go into coarse pitch otherwise your engine is at high risk of disintegration! Do some research on the particular propeller fitted to your airplane as some require an oil accumulator to provide pressure to the governor during any temporary loss of engine oil pressure. The propeller Owner's Manual may yield some useful information.

Section 8 deals with a variety of general knowledge items on the airframe while sections 9 and 10 go into some detail on ancillary systems and instruments. Many of the questions are not applicable to a simple airplane like the Pitts but it is still an excellent education about the type.

I insist on these Endorsement Questionnaires being completed as it obliges trainees to read the manuals for the aeroplane and learn about the systems. One of the most important sections of an AFM or POH is the Limitations so spend some time reading and understanding this. If something is not mentioned there, then it is not a specific limitation.

There is specific information in the checklists and description of normal procedures beyond the generic stuff pilots were taught. The behaviour of oil temperature and pressure just after start is different between a standard Lycoming engine and ours with the inverted oil system.

There is a clear gap between pilot theory training and practical operations which becomes clear when a new pilot completes the questionnaire. Aggravating the issue is the attitude of new pilots who seem to want everything spoon-fed to them – just the brief, essential things of course. They will not bother reading the manuals, perhaps they think it is just like a car where everything is obvious except for some minor things which you can look up in the manual if ever you come across a mysterious switch? They also take absolutely no interest in cockpit placards. They refuse to believe that the designer only puts placards there for very important reasons. The spin recovery placard is one such example and I regularly encounter Pitts pilots who have missed the bit about use of aileron.

Having passed the theory exams and gaining a licence is when the learning really starts. Read the Advisory Circulars and other guidance material as they include lessons learnt from real life experiences. I see pilots do a fuel drain test for water immediately after refuelling but what is the point of that if there has been insufficient time for the water is still suspended in the fuel? "As a guide, the minimum settling time for aviation gasoline is 15 min per 300 mm depth of fuel." Refuel the Pitts as your first job then do the pre-flight inspection and prepare yourself before even thinking of the fuel drain.

5 CESSPIT OF MISINFORMATION

A December 2017 article in CASA's Flight Safety Australia magazine, The Unreachables are they unteachable?, provided this assessment:

How to spot an Unreachable

"I would come to meet many Unreachables, and while it cannot be argued that a great proportion of them were indeed white men over the age of sixty, a surprising number were not: there were females, old and young; pilots of extremely modern aircraft and flying instructors younger than a decent bottle of Scotch. What they have in common, regardless of their age, gender or cultural background, is their implacability; their stubborn resistance of modernity and their steadfast conviction that things were better way back when—they are the human equivalent of t-rex."

I've been called a dinosaur many times for largely that same reason. Not that I resist "modernity" as I have often been at the forefront of advances in knowledge and organizational innovations. But they must be improvements with benefits, not just different and new. I certainly resist modern things which do not provide sustainable and cost-effective improvements and benefits.

I can recall being an MSc student in Professor John Spillman's Aircraft Aerodynamic Design class at Cranfield's College of Aeronautics in 1974 when another student asked "what about biplanes"? Prof Spillman quickly dismissed the subject "That question was resolved 50 years ago!" Yet here we are 50 years further on and aerobatic biplanes are still in production and provide some advantages over monoplanes in this sport.

Their habitat

"Aside from internet forums, chatrooms and message boards, these creatures can often be found grazing at the aero club barbecue. Typically, the alpha of the species will be heard mourning the printed version of the 'crash comics' and insisting that AvFax was a marvelous way to submit flight plans. A word of caution: do approach the alpha carefully and slowly as they can be vicious when attacked. I once had to back away from such a creature when he commenced foaming at the mouth over the topic of aircraft airframe parachutes."

Indeed, those so-called "crash comics", the excellent Aviation Safety Digest is an order of magnitude better than anything you'll see in CASA's Flight Safety Australia magazine. They are all archived on the ATSB's website so you can see for yourself. Macarthur Job, a well known aviation safety expert and writer, was the editor for about ten years commencing in 1967. One of the subsequent editors was David Robson from 1986 to 1988. David went on to build a business, Aviation Theory Centre, including two excellent books which I contributed to:

Aerobatics - Principles and Practice
Three Points – Flying a Tailwheel Aircraft

Incidentally, I also contributed to Bob Tait's excellent book, Tailwheel & Aerobatic Flying.

Mac and Dave shared the attributes as editors of being very knowledgeable and diligent in ensuring a high standard of writing in the magazine. They wouldn't let any misinformation onto their pages.

It went on: "Pack animals, the Unreachables are often seen en masse at safety seminars, fly ins and airshows. Here, the alpha, supported by a small but firm group of 20th century die-hards, will stand and regale the speaker with a lengthy tale of their personal battle with AvMed, even if utterly unrelated to the topic discussed."

Well, discussion of battles with AvMed are very common so where else would people do this except at fly ins and airshows when they get together.

As for CASA safety seminars, well, CASA chooses a few topics to present on but are they really the most important safety topics that pilots want to hear about? As I write this the current topic is "Pushing the envelope"

Using case studies, the seminar explores:

General competency
Fatigue and distractions
Runway incursions
Go arounds"

It is advertised with the comment "An opportunity for industry to interact with us discuss local issues and ask questions". Surely that is an invitation for individuals to raise issues about AvMed. I know that some people do like to hold the floor longer than necessary but perhaps that is because they have been ignored previously and they want people to know they consider it an important issue.

There is more: "If necessary, refer to the facts: modern aircraft are increasingly safety conscious, and contemporary education—now with a focus on human factors and an understanding of human psychology—is aiding our awareness of accident causes and how to avoid them. ... Head-to-head combat very rarely works, and sardonic articles aside, the best procedure for safety promotion is a combination of leading by example—stay current; fly regularly; be present at education awareness seminars; keep an open mind; read blogs, publications and opinion pieces; ask questions of specialist experts and those with more experience than yourself; and remain cheerful and in good humour—never resort to personal insult and mind your manners."

Oh yes, I can't help thinking of a line in the 1944 book, Stick and Rudder, "Almost all fatal flying accidents are caused by loss of control during a turn!" Nearly 80 years later and absolutely nothing has changed. I wonder if that CASA safety seminar will address that?

The paragraph that really struck a chord with me was this one below – "never resort to personal insult", eh?:

"Buoyed by the anonymity of the keyboard, these largely fossilised creatures—with names such as Drunk on AvTur—exist in a cesspit of misinformation, half-baked truths and misshapen facts, fertilised by the manure of their daily postings. It is here the endless threads about 'the myth of the pilot shortage', 'how lift really works' and 'why the government aviation agencies and authority in general must be bashed with a stick' are planted before they spread across aero clubs. It is here where optimism goes to have every beam of light sucked from its cheerful existence. It is here where I learned the difference between fact and opinion."

It is appropriate now to take a look at some of the content of this "cesspit of misinformation" and the origins of it.

The ATSB report of their investigation AO-2017-096 stated:
"In Australia, the Civil Aviation Safety Authority requires the demonstration of recovery from an incipient spin during flight tests. However, there is no clear and consistent definition of the point at which a manoeuvre becomes a spin (or incipient spin) for the purposes of flying training.

Crucially, the ATSB found that there can be varying interpretations of an 'incipient spin', and this has led to aircraft not approved for intentional spins being used for incipient spin training and assessment."

So CASA mandated incipient spins in flight training and pilot licence tests but failed to define what it was they wanted.

"While the ATSB assessed that the instructor's incipient spin recovery knowledge was consistent with established guidelines and did not contribute to the accident, the investigation identified incorrect incipient spin recovery guidance provided by CASA." The Flight Instructor Manual was wrong for many years according to the ATSB – what an abysmal state of affairs.

Another report by ATSB for investigation AO-2014-114 stated:
"The pilot's flight instructor taught and used a method for Chipmunk spin recovery that was reasonably effective in the early stages of a spin, but would become less effective as the spin developed. It was different to the standard method of spin recovery recommended by the Civil Aviation Safety Authority, and to the Chipmunk-specific method recommended by the type design organisation. The flying school's training materials did not include Chipmunk-specific spin recovery methods, and did not clearly emphasise the forward control stick movement necessary for some aircraft."

It makes me angry that a flight instructor could be that incompetent, the flight school so deficient and the regulator who audited them so often could fail.

"The Civil Aviation Safety Authority advised that the flight manual originally produced by the aircraft type design organisation in 2002 was the only currently approved manual for the T Mk 10 Chipmunk in Australia. Records show that the aircraft's flight manual approval lapsed in 2002 and that the newer flight manual was not obtained by the owner. Consequently, pilots of UPD were using information that was out of date. Although there was no requirement for spin recovery guidance to be included, the approved flight manual provided by the aircraft type design organisation did include such guidance and would have provided a reliable source of valuable information for the pilots of UPD to follow.

The flying school had a different flight manual for its Chipmunk aircraft, which was also not approved. Although that flight manual contained generally appropriate spin recovery advice, it did not incorporate the latest approved information. There are variations between aircraft of the same type, often due to modifications and repairs, and using an unapproved flight manual increases the risk that the information within it is not appropriate for that particular aircraft."

There is much to comment on there so let's just consider a few bullet points:
- The flight manual in that aeroplane would've been there since 1956 when it came on the Australian civil register. CASA, or its predecessor, mandated that particular flight manual for a period of nearly 50 years so perhaps the owner thought that it wasn't a big issue?
- Why wouldn't a flight manual be required to include the spin recovery procedure? After all, a flight manual is supposed to include all the information required to safely operate an aeroplane!

An article in those old "crash comics" is especially relevant. There I go again, demonstrating what a dinosaur that I am. The June 1960 article reported on a concern with Chipmunk spin recovery resulting in the Department (a predecessor of CASA) deciding "that each and every Chipmunk aircraft should be spin-tested at maximum all-up-weight and with the centre-of-gravity fully aft, fully forward and neutral." The article described the spin "As in all Chipmunk aircraft the spin entry was not direct and as many as the first four turns were in the nature of a spiral with the airspeed steady at approximately 50 knots after which the nose lifted, the buffeting of the spiral disappeared and the aircraft settled into the true spin at about 45 knots. It was found that this aircraft had three distinct spinning modes characterised by angles of the mean wing chord below the horizon of 24 degrees, 35 degrees and 43 degrees. Each of these angles were achieved on several occasions and in almost all cases it was apparent that a state of equilibrium had been reaches. It is interesting to note that the spinning mode most commonly achieved was the flattest of the three observed (i.e. mean chord 24 degrees below the horizon) and that it was almost the inevitable result of a spin entry using the prescribed standard technique." If only there had been some dinosaurs at that flight school then perhaps the instructors would've known this and the pilot would've been properly trained in spinning the Chipmunk.

The more recent report by the ATSB is also relevant. Investigation AO-2021-025 included Safety Advisory Notice AO-2021-025-SAN-001:

"The ATSB strongly encourages all aerobatic pilots and aerobatic flight instructors to be aware:

- the Mueller/Beggs method of spin recovery does not recover all aircraft types from a spin.
- the Mueller/Beggs spin recovery method limitations should be emphasised during spin theory training.
- the Mueller/Beggs method of spin recovery will not recover a Cessna A150 Aerobat or similar variants from a spin in some circumstances.
- they should review the pilot's operating handbook of the aircraft type that they intend to operate for the recommended spin recovery technique.
- prior to doing spins in any model aircraft, pilots should obtain instruction and or advice in spins from an instructor who is fully qualified and current in spinning that model.

Back in 1975 the FAA published Flight Instructor Bulletin No. 18 in conjunction with Cessna and their document on spinning. It arose from reports of flight instructors having difficulty in recovering from spins in the Cessna 150. The FAA assessed the spin behaviour of a number of examples of the 150 then an FAA officer went around flight schools to address it with instructors.

The NTSB commented on this: "Detailed investigation by the FAA, however, disclosed that problems were related to operational vagaries or anomalies, inadequate knowledge regarding the precise spin recovery procedures for the aeroplane, improper application or misapplication of recovery controls, apprehension, and confusion.

The FAA decided it was necessary to sponsor a stall/spin clinic for instructors run by the US Association of Flight Instructors in 1978. Perhaps this is what is needed in Australia now?

As an engineer I take a keen interest in misinformation related to aircraft structural considerations. This following statement is from CASA's obsolete CAAP 155-1, Aerobatics.

> 3.13.1 Manoeuvring speed (V_A) is the speed above which full deflection of the elevator control will exceed aircraft structural limitations. <u>Below V_A the aircraft will stall before structural limits can be exceeded</u>. V_A will be specified in the aircraft's flight manual and placarded on the instrument panel. Full control deflection of any flight control should be avoided above this speed.

You will see statements like that in many AFMs and it is probably true for that particular aircraft however it is generally not true! Manoeuvering speed, V_A, is determined from its certification by the design regulations FAR 23 and is succinctly explained by the FAA's AC 23-19. First, what it is NOT:

> b. V_A <u>should not</u> be interpreted as a speed that would permit the pilot unrestricted flight-control movement without exceeding airplane structural limits, nor should it be interpreted as a gust penetration speed. Only if $V_A = V_s \sqrt{n}$ will the airplane stall in a nose-up pitching maneuver at, or near, limit load factor. For airplanes where $V_A > V_S \sqrt{n}$, the pilot would have to check the maneuver; otherwise the airplane would exceed the limit load factor.

Some aircraft have a V_A which is more than $V_S\sqrt{n}$ so the pilot must ensure that the limit load factor, n, is not exceeded by taking action even below V_A! Note also that it is not simple even when $V_A = V_S\sqrt{n}$ as it mentions "near, limit load factor".

2.4 SNAPPED MANEUVERS:

> Recent wind-tunnel tests have shown that quick variations of the angle of attack can increase substantially the maximum coefficient of lift of airfoils (unsteady flow). For this reason, the full and quick deflection of the elevator at speeds below or equal to the maneuvering speed (146 mph) can cause the overstepping of the limit load factors and could cause breaking.

This was known many years ago and described in the CAP10B flight manual above.

48. What is the design maneuvering speed V_A?

a. The design maneuvering speed is a value chosen by the applicant. It may not be less than $V_s\sqrt{n}$ and need not be greater than V_c, but it could be greater if the applicant chose the higher value. The loads resulting from full control surface deflections at V_A are used to design the empennage and ailerons in part 23, §§ 23.423, 23.441, and 23.455.

The Pitts S-2B is a good example of this. Stall speed per the POH is 60 mph CAS and the limit load factor is 6. $V_S\sqrt{n}$ = 147 mph CAS however the POH states that V_A is 154 mph CAS! If maximum up elevator at 147 mph results in 6 G then pulling maximum up elevator at the V_A of 154 mph will give you 6.6 G and exceeds the limit load factor!

In 1996 I had the opportunity to conduct some instrumented flight tests in a Pitts S-2B with strain gauges fitted to the fuselage longerons. I also did some finite element structural analysis of the fuselage truss to correlate test results with theory. I slowly built up to where I was doing snap rolls at the maximum recommended speed of 140 mph IAS which is about 139 mph CAS. The accurate instrumentation showed that 6 G was achieved. So, my simple arithmetic indicates that doing the same control actions at the V_A of 154 mph would result in 7.4 G. I heard much later that was indeed what some people were doing with their airplanes – no wonder they were breaking fuselage longerons.

If you have a Pitts S-2C you'll be pleased to hear that we beefed up the fuselage structure.

Finally, a note about V_A for the other model Pitts. The S-1S, S-1T, S-2, S-2A, S-2S, S-2B and S-2C all have a V_A of 154 mph CAS despite their different stall speeds. The applicant gets to choose V_A as not less than $V_S\sqrt{n}$.

Then there are "half-baked truths and misshapen facts" which we should consider. One is airspeed – CAS or IAS?

Earlier versions of FAR 23 required that airspeeds be quoted in CAS for the pilot and that included the markings on the ASI. The Pitts S-2A has a stated stall speed of 58 mph (50 kts), maneuver speed of 154 mph (134 kts) and never-exceed speed of 203 mph (176 kts) – all in CAS. All a bit silly when the ASI displays IAS. Take it to V_{NE} and you'd be 4 kts above the true V_{NE}! Add another 4 kts to my earlier arithmetic related to pulling Gs at V_A.

CASA's predecessor mandated a new Australian-specific flight manual with speeds in kts IAS and associated changes on the ASI. The resulting speeds were stall 55 kts, manoeuvring 130 kts, never exceed 172 kts.

Then in 2001 CASA withdrew those special AFMs and all the aircraft had to revert to the original FAA AFM. But now the markings on the ASI are in IAS so do not conform to the type certificate and differ from the AFM.

Don't ask me which of the above is half-baked and which is misshapen.

The Pitts S-2B also uses CAS as required by FAR 23 but at least the POH includes an airspeed calibration from CAS to IAS. You just need to remember to do the conversion when the POH gives you critical airspeeds in CAS. Add a couple of kts to the take-off and landing speeds for example.

The Pitts S-2C POH is a pleasant surprise with airspeed limitations and performance data in IAS. You also get a calibration table to convert from IAS to CAS. It is interesting that although V_A is 154 mph CAS which is about 156 mph IAS the value in the POH is stated as 154 mph IAS. I guess that they got confused with all of the above.

6 ADVANCED SPINNING

I certainly don't intend for this to be a reference on the subject as there are already several excellent sources of information around, for example, Rich Stowell, Sammy Mason and Gene Beggs. One particularly good set of notes that I like is Spins in the Christen Eagle, an extract from the Christen Eagle II Flight Manual. It has excellent explanations of upright and inverted normal and flat spins however omits the steep accelerated spin modes. As a Pitts aerobatic pilot you must become comfortable at recovering from all inadvertent spin modes and this document provides the essential information. The next higher level to aspire to is to be able to comfortably perform all these spin modes and be able to recognise any mode if entered unintentionally.

As Rich Stowell nicely demonstrates in his videos, the Pitts will readily enter a spin from botched aerobatic manoeuvres. The hammerhead is the most likely culprit with the most common error being to hit the rudder too early, when it has airspeed or excessive kinetic energy, coupled with unwarranted excessive forward stick and excessive opposite aileron. Excessive for that airspeed. A botched Immelmann will also yield a similar outcome.

If you take prompt action to close the throttle and centralise the controls you will remove the forces and moments driving it into the spin. Simply fly away from what happens next

Just to repeat an earlier statement. With power off the Pitts is very docile so that is a clear indication of an essential action if it starts to depart

– close the throttle and fly the airplane. Fly the aeroplane generally means centralising the controls initially. Continue to fly the airplane.

It is not good enough to read about advanced spinning as you must experience it in the company of a good, experienced flight instructor. Check out the website of the International Aerobatic Club for flight schools which specialise in this type of training and then you can be confident that you will gain the skills and knowledge to safely perform aerobatics in a Pitts.

Ensure that your course includes the Beggs-Müller emergency spin recovery procedure. Note also that it does not work for all spin modes in a number of aerobatic aircraft and that includes at least one biplane with "Pitts" in its name.

When done, go back to Cessna's booklet on the Spin Characteristics of their Cessna Models and consider the deeper meaning of that information.

> The final phase is the fully developed "steady" phase. Here, a more-or-less steady state spin results where the autorotational aerodynamic forces (yaw due to rudder deflection, lift and drag differences across stalled wing) are balanced by the centrifugal and gyroscopic forces on the airframe produced by the rotating motion. Due to the attitude of the airplane in a spin the total motion is made up of rolling and usually pitching motions as well as the predominate yawing motions. Movement of the airplane flight controls affects the rate of motion about one of the axes. Because of the strong gyroscopic influences in the spin, improper aerodynamic control inputs can have an adverse affect on the spin motion.
>
> Aileron variations from neutral can cause a different balance between the aerodynamic, inertia and gyroscopic forces and cause some delay in recoveries. Typically even a slight inadvertent aileron deflection in the direction of the spin will speed up rotation and delay recoveries. Moving the elevator control forward while maintaining pro-spin rudder deflection may not provide a recovery with some airplanes. In fact, reversing the sequence of rudder-elevator inputs or even just slow, rather than brisk, inputs may lengthen recoveries. Finally, it is <u>important</u>, particularly in this steady spin phase, in addition to using the correct control application and proper sequence of control application, to HOLD THIS APPLICATION UNTIL THE RECOVERIES OCCUR. In extreme cases, this may require a full turn or more with full down elevator deflection.

Why are some things opposite to the Pitts?

Some of the additional factors which have (or may have) an effect on spin behavior and spin recovery characteristics are aircraft loading (distribution, center of gravity and weight), altitude, power, and rigging.

Distribution of the weight of the airplane can have a significant effect on spin behavior. The addition of weight at any distance from the center of gravity of the airplane will increase its moment of inertia about two axes. This increased inertia independent of the center of gravity location or weight will tend to promote a less steep spin attitude and more sluggish recoveries. Forward location of the c.g. will usually make it more difficult to obtain a pure spin due to the reduced elevator effectiveness. If a spiral is encountered as evidenced by a steady increase in airspeed and

Have a look at my booklet, Learner in a Spin, on Kindle for more information on this subject.

I was fortunate to have worked for a short time alongside James S. Bowman at the NASA Langley Research Center. His Technical Note D-6575, Summary of Spin Technology as related to Light General-Aviation Airplanes, is an important source of information such as the following guidance on primary spin recovery controls as determined by mass distribution.

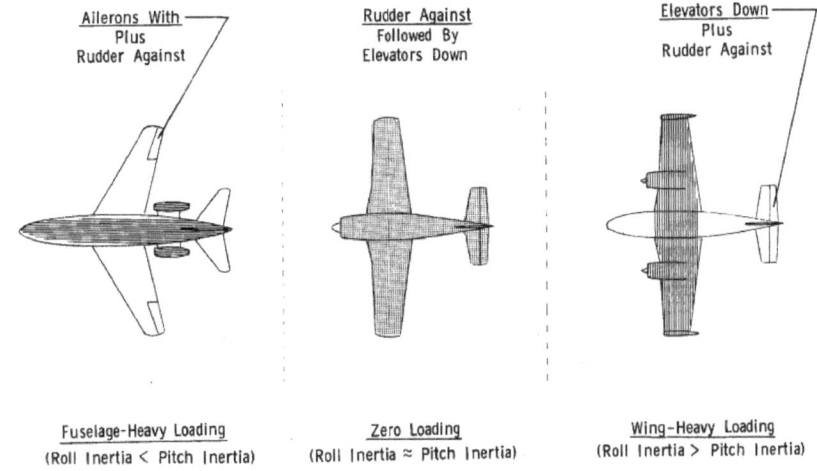

Fuselage-Heavy Loading (Roll Inertia < Pitch Inertia) — Ailerons With Plus Rudder Against

Zero Loading (Roll Inertia ≈ Pitch Inertia) — Rudder Against Followed By Elevators Down

Wing-Heavy Loading (Roll Inertia > Pitch Inertia) — Elevators Down Plus Rudder Against

Also consider Bill Finagin's FART (Finagin's airplane recovery technique) which is even simpler than Beggs-Müller but, again, make sure it will work for your aircraft type before finding yourself having to rely on it. Bill takes the next chapter himself to explain it.

7 TRAIN FOR THE UNEXPECTED

Emergency Recovery, a preferred method, by William B Finagin.

Somehow, we must continue to stress that training for emergency situations is TOTALLY different from doing spin training (which I am very much in favor of as well). People need to understand that when things go badly it is very likely that their brain literally goes into "neutral", and they cannot THINK THEIR WAY OUT of a bad situation.

Allow me two examples of what I am talking about.
1. Would you likely go to a medical doctor who has only read a book on removing a gall bladder for your surgery, knowing that he has never done an operation of that type?

2. Would you get into a Pitts with a pilot who has said that he has never flown a Pitts before this flight and go up to do aerobatics, loops, spins, and inverted flight with him?

I hope your answers would both be a "NO".

First is recognition: All too often things get worse by delaying the correct response or progressing to even doing the wrong thing entirely because they have become confused. But we already know this, however we need to continually stress this to our readers.

Known as Finagin's technique by many but maybe that is it biggest deterrent! Yes, to many it is the FART technique: Finagin's Aircraft Recovery Technique.

Simply the mentioning of the word "pilot" evokes many feelings in our minds, and certainly not one of "bashfulness", "introvert" or even a "wall flower". No, most thoughts go to a self-assured and certainly not a "shrinking violet" individual. As a result, there are those, by their very own nature, who feel that a pilot is sometimes hard to approach if there is a perceived deficiency that could normally be corrected by a straightforward and simple conversation. (Translated this means: pilots are sometimes hard to talk to!)

Over the years many of us have not grasped the difference between two distinctly different entities. This vitally important fact was brought home in an editor's comment in a past IAC magazine article. I quote: "Contest spins and inadvertent spins are two different beasts. Spins that occur due to known control inputs and deliberate action are much easier to recognize and control. Inadvertent spins are much more incapacitating due to their inadvertent nature." Or you might say that one is spin training and the other is "recovery from out of control" situations. One is a planned action and the other an unplanned event. Our brain acts and reacts differently in the two distinctly different situations.

For years we have had the controversy as to "should we teach spins or not teach spins?" Depending on who you talk with or what articles you read you can come down on either side and be justified by the evidence presented. The "cons" point quite correctly to the lowering of fatalities in flight training when the spins were eliminated. One might argue that further examination of the actual evidence may suggest that a high percentage of these accidents occurred at very low levels where they should not have been taught or attempted in the first place. However, there seems to be scant evidence as to the degree of training subsequent pilots involved in spin fatalities ever received in their training.

"Pro" proponents sight the added comfort, if you will, of knowing what will be happening next if given a training curriculum involving spin training. Thus, employing the long-standing axiom of "if you know what will be happening next you will be more in command" and probably thinking more clearly and consequently more likely to make the correct decisions. Doubtful that this changes anything in the brain of a "die-hard" know-it-all pilot with xxxxx number of hours.

However, just hoping that maybe these comments may save at least one life, I will press on.

For years we have read about spin training and spin recoveries and the pros and cons. If one survived, then they obviously touted that method. Eric Müller and Gene Beggs, in my opinion, advanced the survival rate of many by their techniques and I applaud them for their tireless pursuit of success. I hasten to add before going further that I am addressing the recovery from an "out of control" situation where the pilot's brain is mush or at least not in a normal thinking situation. Anxiety, panic, or whatever you choose to call it often distorts how you remember a situation. So, in an "out of control" situation (defined as simply the moment the airplane does not do what you expected the next movement to be) one might argue that previous training in what to do would be very valuable, maybe even "lifesaving".

There is a "mental tunnel vision" that occurs as the student becomes more stressed and his mental field of vision narrows in the sense that he doesn't "record" everything that he sees and recalls only one or two things and not the multiple things he normally monitors. The point being that clear and accurate instruction with multiple reinforcement is one of the essential requirements for an EMERGENCY OR UNPLANNED EVENT.

One must be able to immediately admit to an out-of-control situation, seconds lost in this decision-making event are vital! Next, one must be trained to respond with a rote recall of training to have the best chance of a successful recovery.

So, while some methods in a controlled situation may be faster, it seems logical that IF one had a technique which ALWAYS worked and where you could not make a false move if trained to use the technique then why not use it? Over the years this technique has saved lives, many lives. Simple and idiot proof - IF YOU HAVE RECEIVED QUALITY INSTRUCTION IN THE TECHNIQUE FROM A QUALIFIED INSTRUCTOR!

CAUTION: Do not think reading about it will provide the necessary rote reflex if caught in an "out of control" situation. PLEASE get qualified instruction!

So, what are we talking about? There are four distinct separate steps in the recovery:
1. First, remove ALL the power quickly (we have people say - "RIP OFF THE POWER")
2. Next, FORCE ALL of the controls to neutral and hold them firmly there! (Totally STILL). DO NOT Attempt to fly the airplane!
3. In the Pitts wait for 100 MPH or in other aircraft use 1.4 stall speed value.
4. When you reach 100 MPH pull out of the dive. No matter where you begin your recovery you will ALWAYS be upright at 100 MPH if you have done the previous three things correctly.

Why is this an excellent method? Because you cannot make a mistake by pushing the incorrect rudder or putting the stick in an incorrect position or moving one control before the other one out of sequence. Simple and easy.

In EVERY case in the past thirty years where one has spoken unfavorably of this technique, I have found that they have not tried it with a qualified instructor in the aircraft. So, find a qualified instructor knowledgeable in this technique and give it a whirl. It very well may save your life.

8 SNAP ROLLS

If you were taught aerobatics by me in the Super Decathlon, then you would not know much about snap (or flick) rolls. The wing of the Decathlon is not robust enough to sustain regular snap roll practice so you will probably not find a flight instructor who does it. The Cessna Aerobat on the other hand has no such problem and does very neat snap rolls. Even if you learnt in a Cessna, you may not have been taught snap rolls so the Pitts may be your first encounter with this manoeuvre.

Stomp and yank is essentially the technique. The physics of it are pretty much the same as for a spin but this time I'm not going to bore you with any theory. You already know enough about autorotation and that's all that you need to make the aeroplane do, then stop it abruptly at the right spot. The Cessna Aerobat and Pitts S-1S respond well to a simple stomp (on the rudder pedal) and yank (full back on the control stick or yoke).

Despite it being simple I recommend dual flight instruction for this manoeuvre as there is a safety issue associated with it, the airframe structure discussed in Chapter 4. Another good reason is that it will save time and money to learn quicker rather than floundering around by yourself.

I started you off with the simple stomp and yank method. The S-2C and the S-2A aren't quite as neat in this respect and need to be at the "sweet spot" with respect to the exact timing and rate of control application. The S-2B is even more so where you need to get the stick back and starting to unload it before hitting the rudder. This is another opportunity to point out that we did indeed achieve the design objectives of the model C.

The recommended speed range for snaps is 90 – 140 mph and we are going to use the upper number as a hard limit as we must consider the rolling G limits of the airplane. Furthermore, you can get to the limit load factor of 6 even at speeds around 140 mph despite V_A being 154 mph. Start doing them at the lower end of the speed range because the control forces are lower and the rotation rates and loads on the airframe and pilot are lower. Develop the technique and refine your understanding of that "sweet spot". Start doing them to the left as they will be slower.

Once it has started to roll you should give it aileron in the direction of the roll to accelerate it. At the same time move the stick forward a little to unload it. Here, unload means to reduce the angle of attack which reduces the wing lift so a lower load factor. The effect of unloading is to reduce the drag so as to minimise the airspeed loss during the snap roll. Ensure that you do not unload too much that it unstalls and you are left rolling just because of the applied aileron. Or worse, it transitions to an outside snap roll and much subsequent discussion when back on the ground.

Recovery is a simple matter of reversing the control inputs at the right time. Full opposite rudder, forward stick to unstall and use that aileron to help as well. If you lose control and it is on its way to a spin then also close the throttle and, if necessary, revert to normal spin recovery actions.

Now to refine it, what are the judges looking for? "The judge must see two things to determine that a flick roll has been correctly initiated: a) the aircraft must display a rapid and clearly visible change of pitch attitude to put the wing close to the stall, and b) autorotation must be initiated by use of the rudder. Note that when a flick roll is initiated the angle-of-attack may be at or close to zero (e.g. in vertical and 45 degree lines) or significantly positive or negative if a looping figure is being flown; the pitch change to achieve critical angle-of-attack may thus be less in some circumstances and cannot be fixed. However, if both the required pitch change and actual autorotation are not clearly seen, the figure must be given a Hard Zero (HZ)." There is much more in the rule book but that will give you a good start, hang on for the rest.

The judging rules are quite voluminous and a typical judge at a regional contest can be excused for not being on top of every aspect of the criteria when put on the spot as the manoeuvre happens. However it can be very disappointing for a competitor to be significantly downgraded or even given a zero for something that is clearly not withing the rules. I have seen regional judges noting "buried the snap" as the reason for awarding a zero on the basis that if they were flying the Pitts instead of that pilot they would've unloaded it more. All I can say is protest, unless of course you're at one of those contests where the Contest Director discourages protests and puts an unreasonable cost on protests. Quite unfair for judges to downgrade for considerations which are not described in the rules.

In flying Intermediate Category you will need to fly partial snap rolls as well as snaps on 45° up lines, possibly a half snap on a 45° inverted down line and on the down line of a hammerhead. Considering the snap from straight and level flight as the baseline, the greater the angle of climb the more you must unload it and, the greater the angle of the dive, the less you must unload it.

Half snaps require a quick shift on the rudder just as the roll is stopped to slide the nose back onto the required heading.

One of my favourite party tricks is a one and a half snap from knife-edge to knife-edge. It looks impressive going directly towards the judges or spectators.

9 COMPLEX MANOEUVRES

Moving up to Intermediate after flying Sportsman in a Super Decathlon require mastery of some additional figures prior to attempting the sequences. We've already dealt with snap rolls so next revise some Sportsman Category figures as the Pitts technique may be quite a bit different than what you are used to roll down from stall turn

The upright competition spin will be flown similarly to how we did it in the Super Decathlon but we'll find some complex combinations to contend with. Entry will be the same with the intent to score well and avoid a PZ. Just a few kts above the stall speed, while maintaining horizontal straight flight with the throttle closed, briskly apply full rudder leading the positive application of full back stick and hold it. About 1/3 turn prior to the finish heading apply full opposite rudder and at the instant of reaching that heading briskly apply forward stick. The spin will stop instantly. The judging criteria includes this text "the aircraft must stop rotating precisely on the pre-stated heading, then a 90 degree down, wings-level attitude must be seen." Note the use of the word "then" which means that the vertical attitude with wings level are achieved after the rotation has stopped rather than at the same time that rotation is stopped. Of course, it does look neater if the vertical is achieved apparently instantly and, of course, don't draw a line before achieving the vertical down.

Achievement of that "wing-level" attitude becomes important for spins with ¼ and ¾ turns as the wings will not be level as the rotation stops. As soon as rotation stops you must promptly change the rudder application to eliminate the yaw to get the wings level.

The higher roll rate of the Pitts facilitates many figures and the hammerhead with a ¼ roll down is one of those. No need to reduce power here unlike the Super Decathlon!

In Intermediate you will encounter a push humpty. Instead of a positive loop at the top you will be flying half an outside loop although there will not be much negative G at all. The fact that it is negative G requires further consideration of the different forces and moments involved. At the top of a positive, or inside loop, those same forces and moments tend to cancel one another out when flying the Super Decathlon. Not quite so in the Pitts and definitely not for outside loops. Recall the usual power effects causing roll and yaw to the left. Now add in the gyroscopic effects of the propeller. A pitch up, as with an inside loop, will cause a yaw to the right. Conversely, an outside loop will have a left yaw due to the propeller gyroscopics. Combine the left roll and yaw from the power effects with the left yaw from the gyroscopics means that you must positively apply aileron and rudder to maintain the desired track with wings level. Don't be surprised to run out of aileron at slow speeds here but don't panic, use the fourth control – the throttle. Progressively reduce power as required to maintain control.

Rolling circles are like patting your head with one hand while rubbing your stomach with the other. We'll start in upright straight and level flight and do one inside roll while we turn the airplane through 90° while maintaining constant altitude. By inside roll I mean that the direction of the roll is in the same direction as the turn. The first part of the figure can be likened to rolling into a steep turn. I like to consider each 45° of the turn when describing how to do it, much as I do when describing a barrel roll. Before starting it select a point on the horizon at 45° to the left of the present heading - that is where your nose should be pointing when inverted with wings level. Start to turn left, initially as you would on entering a steep turn (we'll refine this bit later) but maintain aileron to keep rolling and continue to focus on that reference point at 45°. Use rudder and aileron in two different ways. One is to maintain altitude and the other to maintain that rate of change of heading. Upon reaching the 45° immediately select the next one where you will be upright having turned through 90°. Use these same principles to find that you will need to use rudder more aggressively at first to maintain the rate of heading change, then push and again rudder to continue the yaw as you approach wings level.

Now you have some basic idea of what to do you should try holding your model airplane and "fly" it around the room thinking about what you are seeing and what you are doing with the controls at each point. The best way to learn is to have a coach on the ground with a radio while you fly and simply follow your coach's instructions.

Just repeat the cycle and you will get through a full circle with four rolls. That's going to be enough to get you going with Intermediate Category competition.

10 INTERMEDIATE COMPETITION

By the time you get to this chapter you have mastered landing the Pitts and are comfortable flying it around most of the manoeuvres required to compete successfully at the Intermediate level. You've been to contests before in the Super Decathlon so you know the basics but now it is important to learn more about what happens at a contest and why. You will be bullied into doing some judging so take a break from this book now and do an aerobatic judging course because I will assume that you now know all about judging criteria and the basics of figure construction and sequence design. Brush up on this subject in Aerobatics Down Under and then go to the British Aerobatic Association's website for their judging primer at https://www.aerobatics.org.uk/judging

You will need little more more dual flight instruction for you from here on in. You will need a competent coach, who is also an aerobatic judge, on the ground for the most effective training flights. You will find that overhead an aerodrome with an aerobatic box marked out to be ideal for this. Your coach will use a radio as well as a voice recorder. Of course, over an aerodrome there is likely to be other traffic so lookout and communications must be the priority.

Direct coaching by radio while performing the figures can be very effective for certain elements as demanded. For example, when to take action to achieve a length of line or centre the roll on a line. It can also be used for immediate feedback such as lines being off the vertical.

Comprehensive comments recorded by the coach and replayed during debriefing when synchronized with video from the onboard camera is extremely effective at making continual small improvements in technique.

That is the difference between winning and finishing further down the field. Aerobatic competitions are very competitive and are usually won by small margins.

I have seen multiple camera installations however the normal situation for us at Intermediate would be a single action camera. I also see different mounting positions depending on the main objective. A single fixed camera is obviously going to miss a lot of the views required for many figures. A camera mounted on the pilot's head is very useful as it shows what the pilot is looking at which is mostly what is important, or at least more important. Any two-dimensional view will omit information in the other plane which may be vital to improving scores as the judges will be looking. A head mounting may not be practical on a flight helmet or in a tight cockpit.

Regardless, on-board cameras are essential and partly do away with the ground coach as the pilot can self-analyse the flight too.

The next step is to practice the different sequences so as to more closely represent the contest scenario. Work up your Free Known sequence and get feedback from your coach as you develop it.

Let's have a look at a typical Intermediate Free Known sequence that I quickly developed. It has five figures from the Known Master Set for 2020 plus five Free figures for a total of 200 K. The Free figures must be chosen from specific parts of the Catalog to achieve the Versatility requirement of the contest rules.

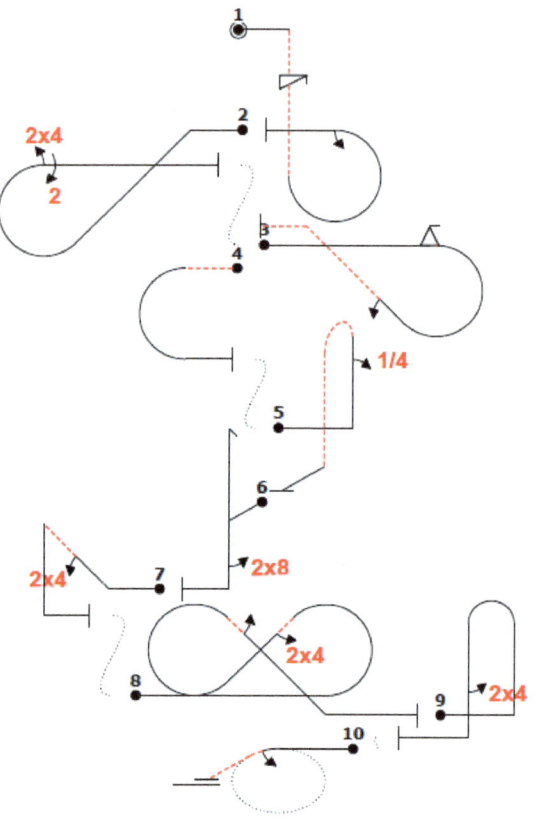

In world championships, not that there are many at this level, the second, third and fourth flights are Free Unknowns. Ten figures are put to the pilots (the process is different for different contests) – each figure must have a minimum of 12 K. Maximum K for each figure is 20. 25 and 30 – it is increased for each flight. Each pilot makes up a sequence comprising those ten figures plus between one and four linking figures of their own choice. Rules specify limits on what can be chosen. Total K factor of the linking figures is taken to be 24 regardless of their actual difficulty.

The CIVA sequences and rules for Intermediate also apply to the Yak-52 category. I've flown a Yak-52 through Sportsman but I wouldn't like to attempt an Intermediate sequence in it as I doubt that I could get enough performance from it without breaking to climb for height. Australian pilot

Russel Sneyd competed in the 2014 World Aerobatic Yak-52 Championships. Russel normally competes in his Yak-54 although he has recently competed in Intermediate with his Yak-52. Other Yak-52 competitors confine themselves to Sportsman.

I found that a Pitts S-2A to be just capable of getting through an Intermediate category sequence within the allotted height and one had to be continuously managing the energy.

At other contests you will encounter other variations so let's just look at one sample Free Unknown on the following page. This is much more challenging than the Free Known on the previous page. Apart from the overall energy required there are some figures there which require a lot of skill for a Pitts pilot.

Figure #5 is a one and a half turn spin with a roll off the top leaving the pilot at low speed. There is no space to accelerate to an ideal speed for #6. A half snap roll to inverted takes much practice to get it to stop in straight and level flight pointing in the right direction! Still not going very fast but now the pilot must immediately do 2 of a 4 point roll, in the opposite direction, to upright flight. It is good that the pilot could not accelerate into #6 as now a low speed is required for #7.

There is a similar segment later. Figure #9 is a roll off the top again leaving the pilot slow. Ideally a much higher speed would suit #10 which is 4 of an 8 point roll followed by a 4 point roll in the opposite direction. The judges will be looking very closely to see which of those points were not spot on. Again, a low speed is required for the following figure.

My opinion is that Intermediate is the category with the most fun! You need a Pitts, or something of similar performance at least, to be able to fly it and that in itself is a lot of fun. The manoeuvres are challenging but not hard on the body so one must put time, effort and money into practice to be prepared for a contest. More fun!

David J Pilkington

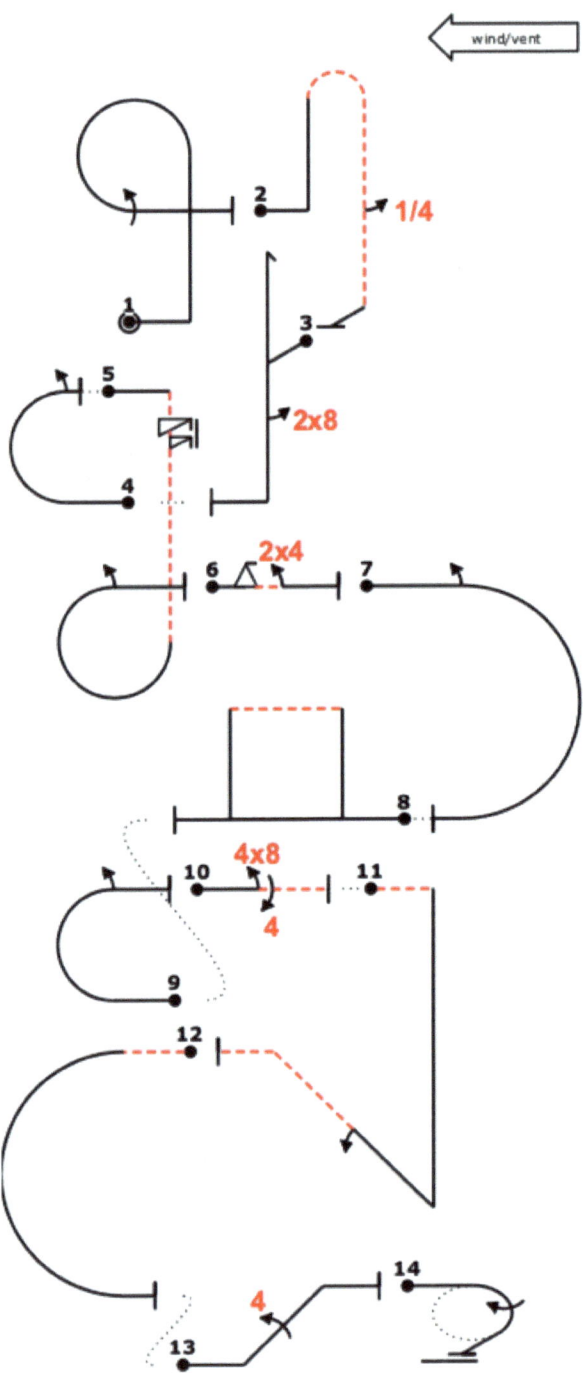

Prepare the aircraft well in advance of the contest and final practice sessions. Ensure that scheduled maintenance completed early if there is a risk of it interfering.

You should take a kit of spare parts and basic tools with you. Screws, spare tube for main tyre, polish, jack to change a tyre. Be prepared to remove spark plugs and clean them. How much can you fit in the baggage compartment of a Pitts?

11 LOW LEVEL AEROBATICS

Australia's Part 61 AERO 1000 flight activity endorsement authorises a pilot to conduct aerobatic manoeuvres above 1,000 ft AGL. A prerequisite is the AERO 1500 endorsement as described in my book Aerobatics Down Under. An AERO 1000 endorsement is required to compete at Intermediate Category level in Australia.

The USA's International Aerobatic Club has a lower limit of 1,200 ft for Intermediate whereas the normal minimum height for acrobatics in the USA is 1,500 ft. The rules and exemptions in the USA are substantially different than in Australia and are generally less prescriptive yet the accident rate is at least as good. There is no requirement for an aerobatic endorsement and no requirement to be trained by an aerobatic instructor before conducting solo aerobatics. The USA requires a waiver for an Aerobatic Practice Area for those pilots operating below 1500 ft. The only qualification required of the pilot is membership of the IAC.

Aerobatic display pilots in the USA need an annual assessment for their approval to perform low level aerobatics. That is much more tightly controlled than the Australian system of a permanent aerobatic endorsement down to 500 ft or down to ground level.

The Part 61 Manual of Standards for the AERO 1000 endorsement is identical to that for the AERO 1500 endorsement so what is different? Just my opinion that you must demonstrate competence and safety in performing the privileges of that endorsement. So that means flying Intermediate Category sequences rather than Sportsman.

"Design an aerobatic routine".

- My syllabus uses the CIVA Intermediate requirements for the design of a Free Known sequence and a Free Unknown sequence. Pilots would use the free online software OPENAERO to do this. CASA goes on: "involve practical transitions between manoeuvres, and identify performance parameters that will ensure safe completion of all manoeuvres not below 1,000 ft AGL". 1000 ft is 2/3 numerically of the previous endorsement however the considerations increase exponentially rather than linearly.
  - Then CASA requires "performance parameters ... that provide go-no go guidance for safe completion of all manoeuvres". Less margin for error so much more important here, especially as we are flying a higher performance aeroplane conducting more complex manoeuvres.
- "Plan an aerobatic performance". The Free Known sequence can be done at leisure but the Free Unknown sequences must be developed and planned at the contest in a small window of time with the pressure of the competition. We'll use the Unknown sequence requirements to demonstrate this competency.
  - "identify the stakeholder requirements ... plan to safely present the sequence".
  - "required aerobatic approvals" a number appropriate to the contest, most organized by the contest officials but it is the pilot's responsibility to comply with the rules. I have seen CASA rules and exemptions which the contest officials blithely instruct the pilots to ignore!
  - "plan manoeuvres to remain in the box"
  - "recall and apply the go-no go performance criteria". Particularly difficult for an Unknown sequence when it is likely that the pilot has not previously flown a manoeuvre and there is no opportunity to practice.
  - "recall escape manoeuvres"

My training syllabus for the AERO 1000 aerobatic endorsement would expect to take about 16 hours of solo flying with some coaching from the ground and by video observation. A prerequisite is the Pitts checkout including dual training in advanced spins.

First practice the core manoeuvres – upright spins, inverted spins, upright level snap rolls, snap rolls on 45- and 90-degree lines up and down, inverted turn, vertical rolls, rolling circles and some negative G figures.

Next is development and practice of the CIVA Free Known sequence. Practice high initially, above 3,000 ft AGL and slowly work lower. Remember that the judges can be quick to award low altitude penalties so don't plan to go lower than 1200 ft AGL.

You'll need to develop and fly some Free Unknown sequences in simulated contest scenarios. Again, start and finish much higher than the competition lower limits in your initial training. The assessment flight will be a Free Unknown sequence flown in a competition scenario.

The theory includes a detailed revision of the basic aerobatic endorsement's underpinning knowledge then the additional elements for the AERO 1000 endorsement. A fairly comprehensive written knowledge assessment as you'll need to know this stuff to fly safely. Things such as:
- Significance of stick position with respect to spin recovery.
- Factors which may lead to a flat spin.
- Difference between an upright and inverted spin.
- Mueller-Beggs spin recovery action and limitations on its application.
- Airspeed limitations ... V_A and rolling G limitations.
- Physiological effects of positive and negative G.
- The effects of sustained and rapid changes of G loading.
- Energy management as applied to aerobatic routines.

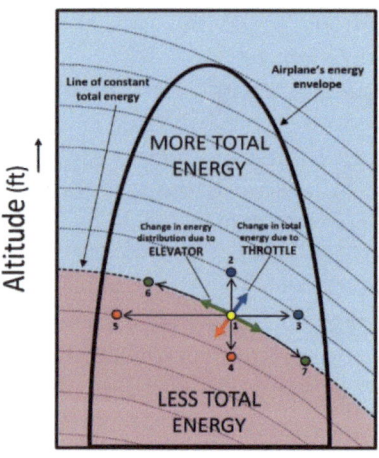

The FAA's Airplane Flying Handbook has a new Chapter 4, Energy Management: Mastering Altitude and Airspeed Control which is a good place to start reading on this subject.

Then move on to Rich Stowell's excellent article: A Pilot's View of Energy Management!

12 ADVANCED COMPETITION

The contest process is much the same as for Intermediate however the complexity and difficulty of the figures is increased significantly. If you've been flying a Pitts S-2A in Intermediate Category you would know it has reached its performance limit and you will need to move on. Any of the single seat Pitts with four ailerons or an S-2C are your options here. We'll discuss the use of an S-2C.

The minimum height for Advanced Category is 200 m or 660 ft AGL so you will need an AERO 500 endorsement to compete. The standard required is to demonstrate competency and safety at flying the various competition sequences. The underpinning knowledge is similar to that for the AERO 1000 endorsement with one additional item: "potential danger associated with conducting aerobatics at 500 ft AGL over unfamiliar terrain." The short story with that is do not fly over unfamiliar terrain!

There is an additional competency element specified in the MOS: "demonstrate safe behaviour". A good way to meet that requirement is to have conducted regular safety peer reviews as described in my book, Aerobatics Down Under.

The most important aspect of the 500 ft endorsement is that the lower limit is very much closer to the ground and will be overwhelming at first. Work lower in stages. Do some very simple independent figures from a base of 500 ft AGL to get the sight picture. Descending to 500 ft there is little time to refer to the altimeter and it lags as well. You must judge your height visually.

As with Intermediate you will fly a Free Known sequence and several Free Unknown Sequences. The British Aerobatic Association provides a default Free Known sequence for you to get started with. They also provide a .seq file that you can use with OpenAero. An example is shown on the following page.

This is quite a challenging sequence for a Pitts so develop the skills first by flying segments of the sequence. The first time that you fly it all the way through you should be fairly comfortable with each individual figure and know the gate for each. Recall the gate:

- Airspeed – know the maximum end minimum entry speed.
- Altitude - decide the minimum entry altitude for each figure - plan the altitude at each point in the sequence.
- Where are the judges – can you see them?

Once you get through the sequence safely you can start refining the technique to optimise your score. You must be as familiar with the judging criteria as the Chief Judge.

ADVANCED AEROBATICS DOWN UNDER

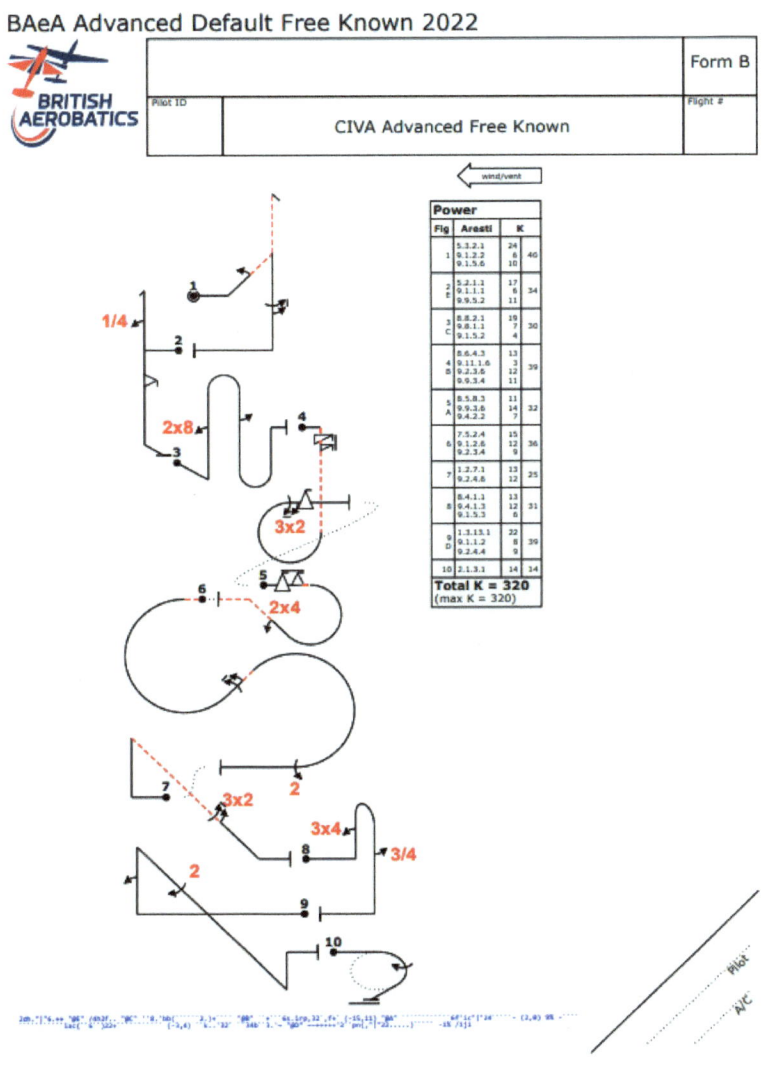

If you don't understand or agree with what is said at the pilot briefing then ask. That text on the slide below in red is not correct per the current AAC rules, is it?

Rolling Turn Downgrades

ii) Where continued rolling is seen to bring the wings level after the turn is completed the following deduction should be applied:

- Less than 15 degrees of roll is executed: 1 point
- Between 15 degrees and 30 degrees of roll is executed: 2 points
- Between 30 degrees and 45 degrees of roll is executed: 3 points
- More than 45 degrees of roll is executed: PZ

Note that this is where the usual 1 point for every 5 degrees does not apply.

The Free Unknowns are much more challenging as you don't have any opportunity to practice the sequence and may not have even flown some of the figures presented to you. Let's see how Bruno Roque dealt with the first Free Unknown at the 2022 Victorian Aerobatic Championships. We'll dissect his planning of this sequence below.

The table on the right identifies the figures he was presented with by the alphabetic characters A, B, C etc. The pilot added his own linking figures identified by "Add." The Aresti catalog numbers and K are shown too. Any additional figures added only earn a total K of 8 so that all pilots have the same total K for their sequences.

That string at the bottom of the page specifies the sequence for the OpenAero app.

Figure #8 obviously provides half of a crosswind corrector pair of figures and it is positioned reasonably well just after halfway through the sequence. I would prefer an earlier place as the preceding 7 figures take much more time subjected to drift in any crosswind. However, it does ensure an accurate positioning to impress the judges for the last 4 figures. Figure 1 may have also been used as a crosswind corrector however it does not pair with the hammerhead due to the differences in entry and exit speeds.

That spin then logically starts the sequence as it loses the most height and the Pitts' performance enables the rest of the sequence to be flown at the ideal positioning for the judges.

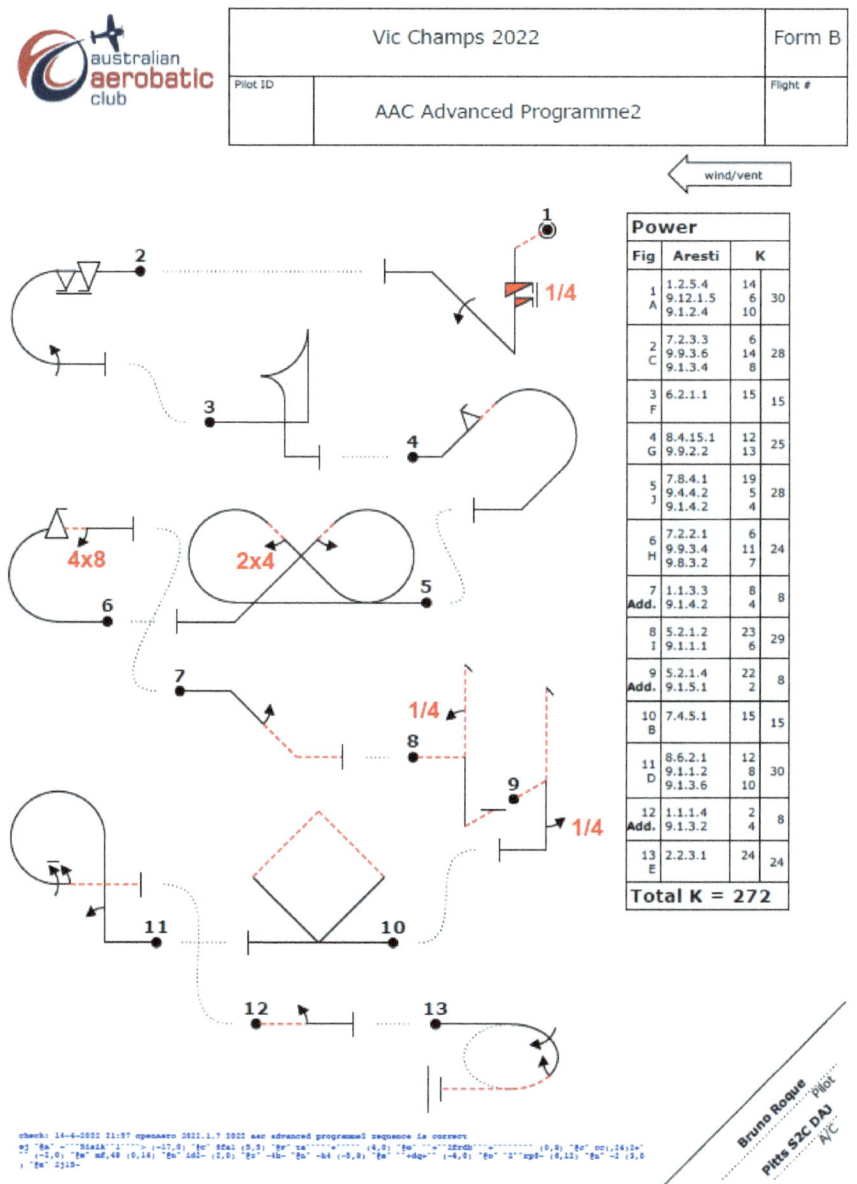

Entering the box on the Y axis requires accurate positioning otherwise you'd wish that the crosswind correction had been placed much earlier.

Remember that spins are notoriously difficult to start in the right place in the sky!

My guess is thar the pilot then identified some figures that he was less comfortable about them scoring well and put them next in the sequence.

Figure 2 works well where it is situated. At the end of that he was down to about 2,000 ft.

A tailslide is always at risk of going the wrong way or otherwise displeasing the judges so it is a good choice to have it as figure #3 where it is quite high in the sky.

The top is 2800 ft and he finishes the figure at 1700 ft.

The S-2C is fast and takes up a lot of sky. The pilot needs to conserve energy and typically flies at 160 mph, or 140 kts, between manoeuvres which is an adequate entry speed for many of these figures. That is less than the maximum straight and level speed so it is accelerating or gaining energy. The Advanced sequence is tough going for the S-2C and the flight must be planned with energy conservation in mind.

Figure 4 is a neat turnaround figure. The instrumentation tells us that Bruno has been flying to conserve energy. He has only pulled a maximum of 4 G with -2 G from the inverted spin.

Pilots do not enjoy horizontal eights such as figure #5. There are too many elements and 45-degree lines which enable judges to readily downgrade the score. It has a fairly high K factor too so those point reductions really hurt.

If the attitude indicator is not aligned exactly with the horizon the judges will see it. The pilot cannot correct it as the judges will then have their opinion confirmed! Get it right the first time and hold that attitude to earn top scores.

The pilot is now down to 1500 ft in figure #6. Point rolls also enable the judges to downgrade a pilot's score. A full positive snap roll from inverted flight is hard enough to score well at without adding half an 8-point roll to it.

Figure #7 was a good choice to select to set up for the hammerhead with an inverted entry. On this day the pilot used the crosswind corrector pair well to position himself for the final segment.

Down at 1200 ft for the half roll right in front of the judges.

Ideally, it would've been a bit lower however the planning must be conservative as there is no practice. Better to be higher rather than risk running out of energy at the bottom of the box and having to break.

Turn away from the judges in the final figure, a rolling circle, as the pilot knows that the roll will be good, and the judges will be picky with the roller so move away a bit.

Bruno Roque won that 2022 contest with a score of 65.677% overall. His score for the flight described above was 80.176% - great work - congratulations!

13 FORMATION AEROBATICS

A change of pace with this chapter to finish off. The aerobatics itself is generally fairly simple however extreme precision is obviously required so working up to an AERO 500 endorsement prior to tackling this may be appropriate.

Of course, you must be proficient at flying formation generally as well before you even think of starting formation aerobatics. The documentation provided at http://www.flyfast.org/ is excellent as a refresher. "The Formation and Safety Team (FAST) is a worldwide, educational organization dedicated to teaching safe formation flying in restored, vintage military aircraft and civilian aircraft."

I learnt formation flying in a Cessna 150 and the Cessna is still popular with aero clubs as a formation trainer. The FAST material is based on low wing aircraft, so you'll have to adjust some parameters accordingly. Like many, I believe that a low wing type is preferable for formation flying due to the visibility up and around. The Cessna has some blind spots which must be identified and allowed for when flying.

My preferred type for basic formation flying is one of the 150 hp variants of the Airtourer. There used to be a group of people at Moorabbin Airport flying formation as a team, including formation aerobatics, in 115 hp Airtourers. The military trainer development of it, the CT-4 Airtrainer is also very suitable.

The Pitts is also excellent in formation flying and formation aerobatics. The only disadvantage is the blind spot created by the top wing but it is not a major problem and you can easily allow for it. A word about takeoff and landing – especially the latter. With the tail down the visibility ahead is abysmal and, coupled with the concentration required for a pilot to control it on the ground, there is added risk of collision. In fact, there have been numerous collisions. Do stream takeoffs and landings with a good spacing of 5 seconds for takeoff and 10 seconds for landing. After landing follow the detailed pre-flight briefing on what you will do to minimise any risk.

Harry Markby, Ken McKechnie and Ron Aspin were all military fighter pilots in WW2. In the late 1970s they started flying formation aerobatics together.

Harry joined the RAAF in June 1941, at the age of 18, gaining his wings and a commission in March 1942. He was a Hawker Typhoon pilot with No. 174 Squadron RAF and commanding officer in 1944. Harry took part in the audacious air raid on Amiens Prison on February 18, 1944, which famously sought to free jailed members of the French resistance. He was subsequently awarded the Distinguished Flying Cross. He was a foundation committee member of the Australian Aerobatic Club Melbourne Chapter.

Ron Aspin flew Corsairs with the USN. He built his own Pitts S-1E and competed in Unlimited Category competitions. I remember judging his flight in either 1981 or 1982 at the Australian Nationals. Competition was tough for team selection for the World Championships and he needed every point to make the last spot. I gave him zero, along with the other judges, for his tailslide and he remonstrated to me about it. He said it was a beautiful tailslide, just like he had been doing in his practice flights. My response was that he had obviously been practicing it wrong all year. His slide recovery went the wrong way!

Ken McKechnie was the foundation President of the Australian Aerobatic Club and foundation committee member of the Australian Aerobatic Club. It was largely through Ken's efforts that the Melbourne Chapter raised sufficient funds to purchase a Pitts S-2A and a Pitts S-1C. Ken flew Mustangs towards the end of WW2 but did not see service.

Newton Sanbrook was also instrumental in the Club's purchase of the Pitts aircraft.

The Pitts S-1C needed 4 ailerons for those of us keen on competition flying. Ron Aspin had the facilities and knowledge after building his aeroplane so took the lead. The Club purchased an S-1E wing kit from the factory and we converted the S-1C to an S-1E.

I had designed new symmetrical ailerons with spades for the Pitts for Frank Fry and Bill Waterton Jr to help improve the performance of their Pitts for the 1980 World Championships. This was in the days before Experimental Category in Australia so the work required was the same as for an STC. It was a substantial effort by myself. The ailerons performed to our expectations and no redesign was necessary. Ken McKechnie did the required spin tests.

Harry resigned as leader of the formation aerobatic team and I took his place in 1979 flying the Club's S-2A, VH-SZA. Ken flew the Club's S-1E, VH-DDS, and Ron flew his own S-1E, VH-WIZ. My first display was at the Calder racetrack in March and we did many regular displays at that venue. We also did displays at many local airshows over the next two years.

Our Calder displays would start with me dropping Vikta Klein out of the front seat for him to parachute down onto the car racetrack in front of the spectators. I would slowly (for a Pitts) roll inverted and give it a tad of forward stick to allow Vikta to exit gracefully.

I would then rejoin the two S-1s and start the formation display diving straight at the crowd. During the dive I would do a slow roll as Ken and Ron stayed in vic formation. I must admit they widened out the first few times I did it. Most of our display comprised barrel rolls and loops in that same vic formation with simple climbing turnarounds. We also did a hammerhead in echelon right formation. For one segment I would pair with Ken for an inside-outside loop with Ken doing the hard work of the negative G. Ken and Ron would pair off for a duo including hammerheads at opposite ends of the crowd with opposing snap rolls as they pass in opposite directions. We would rejoin to finish with a Prince of Wales feather then rejoin as we departed the scene.

Rob Fox's excellent photography made the front page of The Age newspaper in 1980.

As you can see, we all wore parachutes as risk mitigation.

1979 was when I gained my 500 ft aerobatic approval, equivalent to the AERO 500 endorsement, and commenced flying Unlimited Category sequences.

I had too many other commitments to devote adequate time to formation aerobatic practice and displays. We had just started to build our homebuilt Laser and I wanted to focus on that to get into serious aerobatic competition. There was still time for fun, however.

The Club organized a competition with everyone flying Sportsman Category. As I dived in with the Pitts S-1E I thought that it was a bit tame after flying Unlimited so on the spur of the moment I rolled inverted, did the 3 wing dips, and did an outside loop instead of an inside loop. It caused some consternation on the judging line. Even more consternation when they realized that I was flying the whole sequence inside-out. I was fine up until the snap roll when it dawned on me that I'd never done an outside one before – however it worked out fine.

www.ingramcontent.com/pod-product-compliance
Lightning Source LLC
Chambersburg PA
CBHW042327150426
43193CB00001B/10